D1400751

Churchill's Last Wartime Secret

This book is dedicated to my two-year-old grand-daughter, Hannah, the perfect tonic for a long-distance writer struggling to get across that elusive finishing line!

Churchill's Last Wartime Secret

The 1943 German Raid Airbrushed from History

Adrian Searle

Pen & Sword
MILITARY

First published in Great Britain in 2016
and reprinted in 2017 by
PEN & SWORD MILITARY
An imprint of
Pen & Sword Books Ltd
47 Church Street
Barnsley, South Yorkshire
S70 2AS

ISBN 978 1 47382 381 5

A CIP catalogue record for this book is
available from the British Library

Typeset in Ehrhardt by
Mac Style Ltd, Bridlington, East Yorkshire

Printed and bound in England by
CPI Group (UK) Ltd, Croydon, CR0 4YY

Pen & Sword Books Ltd incorporates the Imprints of Aviation, Atlas,
Family History, Fiction, Maritime, Military, Discovery, Politics, History,
Archaeology, Select, Wharncliffe Local History, Wharncliffe True Crime,
Military Classics, Wharncliffe Transport, Leo Cooper, The Praetorian Press,
Remember When, Seaforth Publishing and Frontline Publishing.

For a complete list of Pen & Sword titles please contact
PEN & SWORD BOOKS LIMITED
47 Church Street, Barnsley, South Yorkshire, S70 2AS, England
E-mail: enquiries@pen-and-sword.co.uk
Website: www.pen-and-sword.co.uk

Contents

Acknowledgements

Any acknowledgement for the help and support I have received in writing this book must start with my publishers, Pen & Sword, for entrusting me with the task of uncovering the truth behind the enduring 'raid on the radar' wartime legend – despite the handicap of having little in the way of archival material to consult owing to the continuing insistence by the British Government that the story I was setting out to tell had no verifiable factual basis. Put another way, there was nothing officially available to prove it *was* a fact! I very much appreciate the faith which Pen & Sword have vested in my ability to crack the toughest nut of a writing assignment I have yet to undertake – and I especially appreciate the patience extended to me by Heather Williams in the editorial and production team when I have asked – more than once – for a little more time!

I must also express my gratitude to my editor (and fellow Isle of Wight resident) Carol Trow, whose perceptive professionalism undoubtedly has enhanced the final presentation of this work.

The support of family is always a tremendous help, especially when, as with my son, Matt, and daughter-in-law, Sarah, they are able to contribute directly to the book with photography and mapping respectively. The encouragement of other family members is also acknowledged while special thanks are extended to Mark Steadman and Ashley Webb here in my home town of Ryde. Their extraordinary enthusiasm for the project and the practical help they have provided with the research has been of tremendous value over a long period of time. The support I have received regularly from Roger Bunney has also proved an immense help.

The Isle of Wight is at the heart of the story told in this book. Countless people on the island have willingly given their time and the benefit of their knowledge in the realms of raid folklore. Most are acknowledged within the book's narrative but special thanks must be extended to Gareth Sprack for sharing the incredible story of his chance meeting in France with a German ex-serviceman who, as it turned out, seems actually to have been a member of the wartime raiding party at St Lawrence in 1943! Both Gareth and his wife, Val, have also provided valuable insights into other aspects of the story. I am immensely grateful for their help which was so freely given.

Which brings me to Alfred Laurence who, more than twenty years ago, first revealed to me the details of the hushed-up raid he had gleaned from his good friend in Germany, Dietrich Andernacht, another apparent member of the wartime enemy's raiding party. Both men have since died but their joint contribution to fleshing out the bones of the story was immense, indeed pivotal. There wouldn't have been a book without them. Alfred, or Fred as he was known during his days as an Isle of Wight resident, had led a truly remarkable life (worthy of a book in itself) and I warmly acknowledge the enormous input of his USA-based son Geoffrey in helping me to piece together the extraordinary story of the man who, in retirement, had devoted much of his energy to the quest of establishing the wartime raid as a fact.

With a paucity of nationally archived material available, much of the formal research for the book has been undertaken on the island, from where invaluable records have emerged to support the evidence from Germany. The dedication and friendly service extended at the Isle of Wight Record Office in Newport always makes the task of carrying out research there a pleasure. Some of the strongest documentary evidence used in the book was the product of the hours I spent in the office. It was also a pleasure to carry out research at Carisbrooke Castle's wonderfully evocative museum while secreted among the maze of high-level rooms which make up the old Norman stronghold's inner sanctum. My thanks to the curatorial staff there for going out of their way to meet my requests for inspecting material relevant to the book.

In the south of the island I received an immediate response from Ventnor & District Historical Society's Michael Freeman to my request for information on the town's wartime and post-war doctors in a bid to discover who might have been at the heart of a story relayed to Gareth Sprack about a local GP who apparently discovered medical notes relating to raid casualties – but was then seemingly warned off his quest for further information by high authority. This strand of the 'raid on the radar' legend remains a work in progress which can hopefully be pursued in the near future with further help from Ventnor's excellent historical group.

At the island's southernmost point I was readily granted out-of-season access by Trinity House to the lighthouse at St Catherine's and the chance to inspect its wartime records which are preserved on site. Special thanks go to Andrew Booth, the lighthouse's visitor centre tour guide, for turning out on a windswept December morning to accommodate my search for the facts.

Further south, I was grateful to the wartime historians of the Channel Islands Occupation Society in Guernsey for sparing the time to talk to me and helping to clarify some key issues. In the fascinating nearby island of Alderney – a personal favourite – on a, literally, flying visit it was a pleasure to spend time with the Alderney Society's Dr Trevor Davenport discussing possible links between his island and a German raid nearly seventy-four miles to the north.

In Germany a great deal of help was readily provided by Silvia Stenger and archival colleagues at Frankfurt in my attempts to trace as much information as possible about former city archivist Dietrich Andernacht. I should also acknowledge the help of the country's national archival service, the *Bundesarchiv*, as I sought to uncover any details of the raid which might survive among the documents in their possession. The staff there offered a lot of potential leads but, with no precise knowledge of the incident, were unable to pin the story down.

Back in England, days at both the National Archives in Kew (which did yield a few things of relevant note) and the RAF Museum in Hendon were made the more pleasurable by the kindness and professionalism of their respective staffs – though it takes a lot of effort when at Hendon to pull oneself away from the magnificent collection of aircraft and head back to the desk!

Several regional and regiment-specific military museums and associations were consulted. I am grateful for the guidance they have each provided, in particular Major Hugo White at Cornwall's Regimental Museum in Bodmin and Lieutenant Colonel Michael Motum at The Rifles office in Taunton for their help with the relevant wartime histories of, respectively, the 7th Battalion Duke of Cornwall's Light Infantry and the 5th Battalion Somerset Light Infantry.

It is not possible to name everyone who has helped the development of this project. There have been so many. But I sincerely appreciate their assistance. I hope they will enjoy the book.

Adrian Searle
July 2016

Preface

This book tells the story of something which never happened! That, at least, is what the British Government would have us believe. It has been its official stance on the matter ever since the Second World War. Consistently, the Ministry of Defence and the Home Office have insisted that, despite the many rumours to the contrary, no part of the British mainland shuddered under the weight of jackboots worn by German forces engaged in active military service. Or, at least, if it *did* happen, there is absolutely no official documentary evidence to prove it.

The term 'mainland' in this context is taken to mean all component parts of the UK and, while this excludes the German-occupied Channel Islands to the south, it does, of course, include the Isle of Wight. However, the isle would beg to differ. Since the defeat of Nazi Germany in 1945 the story has been told of a seaborne enemy attack in the mid-war years on one of the island's RAF radar stations. For many of the generation living in the immediate post-war years in the south of the Wight, the story was regarded as a truism. No big deal.

Yet, if it really did happen, it would clearly have been a big deal at the time and, symbolically at least, it would be a pretty big deal today if it could be confirmed. The wartime history books would need revision. Britain's shores had not remained inviolate to an enemy landing after all.

But such stories are common, enshrined in local folklore in several parts of the country. What makes this one so special, so distinctively different to all the others? This book sets out to answer that question with as much evidence as the total lack of official corroboration would allow. The usual national archival sources have largely had to be discounted during an extended period of research. There is not going to be anything of use archived – it did not happen.

Yet there can be little doubt that it did and, for the first time in the burgeoning chronicles of German landing stories from the 1939–45 war, the most persuasive evidence comes not from the British side of the wartime divide but from the German perspective. It is compelling material and, supported as it is to a large degree by other evidence, both written and verbal, it will hopefully prove sufficient to convince even the most sceptical of readers to accept it as fact.

This book does not seek to cast a critical shadow over the memory of Winston Churchill or to impugn in any way his extraordinary qualities as a wartime leader. It is hard to argue against the notion that imposing a veil of secrecy in Britain over a mid-war enemy attack on the Isle of Wight was entirely justified. But why does this remain a secret today? The Second World War was won. Nothing is going to change that. After more than seventy years it is time for a proper investigation into the truth behind the rumours of what happened on the island in 1943.

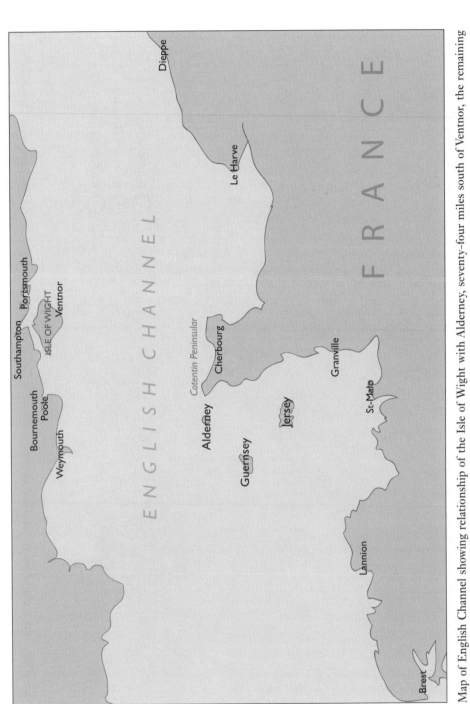

Map of English Channel showing relationship of the Isle of Wight with Alderney, seventy-four miles south of Ventnor, the remaining Channel Islands and the northern French (Brittany and Normandy) coast. (*Sarah Searle*)

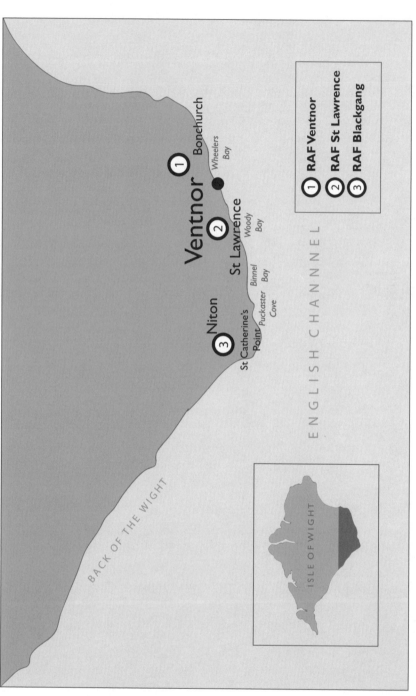

Map of the southern tip of the Isle of Wight showing positions of the Ventnor area's three wartime RAF radar stations. (*Sarah Searle*)

Chapter 1

The Rumour Mill: Flaming
Seas and Bodies on the Beach

T hat the Isle of Wight is not alone as a suggested location for a hushed-up seaborne German incursion onto British soil during World War Two can be described as a masterpiece of understatement. It is one among a great many. Ever since the cessation of hostilities in 1945 rumours of enemy landings have persisted, particularly around the eastern and southern coasts of England, to challenge the proud assertion that no German forces engaged in military action set foot on British soil (the Channel Islands excepted) throughout the six years of conflict.

To eliminate the potential for confusion, this statement does not include enemy aircrew shot down over Britain who resisted arrest by firing on those sent to detain them. There were incidents of this kind on the Isle of Wight although probably the most famous example was the so-called Battle of Graveney Marsh in Kent which occurred on the night of 27 September 1940 between the crew of a downed Junkers Ju-88 bomber and a detachment of soldiers from the 1st Battalion of the Royal Irish Rifles – popularly recorded as the last engagement with a foreign force to take place on mainland Britain but hardly qualifying as a planned enemy attack.

Many of these tales tell of an allegedly failed operation, with the enemy repulsed before they could reach dry land. Most are set against the backdrop of British vulnerability to seaborne attack in the summer of 1940. Despite their exposure in recent times as probable myths, products of 'black propaganda' conceived in, and strategically distributed from, the UK for targeted international consumption, some of these tales have gained an air of reliability and apparent veracity thanks to the inclusion of dramatic detail, supposed hard evidence and a heady dose of whimsical imagination. Something of a cause célèbre among these is the enduring story of an attempted Nazi invasion at the tiny Suffolk fishing village of Shingle Street.

Located twelve miles east of Ipswich at the mouth of Orford Ness, Europe's largest vegetated shingle spit, there is today little of particular note at once prosperous Shingle Street. The hamlet is primarily known for its holiday homes and its proximity both to the nature reserve on the Ness and, just over two miles away, the men's prison and young offenders' institution at Hollesley Bay, still referred to locally as Hollesley Bay Colony (or simply, The Colony), which opened as a Borstal in 1938. At the outbreak of war a year later, Shingle Street did at least have a pub, the Lifeboat Inn. By the end of the conflict the pub had been flattened, its demise a component of the mysterious German invasion stories that developed in post-war years.

Orford Ness lies in the background of that mystery. Before the arrival of National Trust stewardship in 1993, following land purchase from the Ministry of Defence, the Ness was steeped in secrecy. During both world wars and beyond, the Ministry and its predecessors utilised the out-of-the-way peninsula for a variety of experimental military activity. This included its use for examining the potential for a flying field on marshland before, in 1929, the area began serving as a test-bed location for the development of the Orford Ness Beacon, an early experiment in long-range radio navigation. In operation from July of that year, the beacon was housed in a small building resembling the lower portion of a Dutch windmill. Painted black (and thus referred to colloquially as the Black Beacon), it remains in situ today as a striking reminder of Britain's pioneering pre-war development of radio navigation systems.

The trail-blazing beacon was followed by the installation of purpose-built equipment on the Ness for initial evaluation by the remarkable Scottish engineer Robert Watson-Watt, heading a small, personally chosen team, of the revolutionary radio direction finding (RDF) principle.[1] Eventually adopting a user-friendly term originated by the United States Navy, the system would famously be developed as radar (an acronym for what the Americans called radio detection and ranging) to give Britain a crucial defensive shield in the dark days of war. Despite an initial element of high-level political and military doubt over RDF's likely effectiveness against perceived aerial threat, the team's research was moved in 1936 to a new base at Bawdsey Manor, fifteen miles to the south, following its purchase by the Air Ministry. It was at this imposing nineteenth century neo-Jacobean house that the first link in the Chain Home (CH) radar network destined to prove so vital in the Battle of Britain was built. Fully operational by September 1937, it spawned the development of a comprehensive chain which included at its western extremity a station atop St Boniface Down on the Isle of Wight.

Watson-Watt's remarkable research group was dispersed elsewhere two years later on the outbreak of war with Germany but Bawdsey's radar site continued to operate – as RAF Bawdsey – throughout the conflict while the chain was modified and expanded to meet the threat.[2]

What went on in utmost secrecy before and during World War Two at Orford Ness, Bawdsey Manor and the fifteen miles of coastline in between was bound to lead to post-war speculation. Such rumours will always benefit when, as at Shingle Street, there were very few around aside from the military to bear verifiable eyewitness testimony. During 1940, in the wake of the fall of France and amid heightened invasion scares in Britain, the whole of the East Anglian shoreline from King's Lynn down to Southend-on-Sea was designated a coastal defence area. The repercussions were profound. Well in excess of 100,000 residents were uprooted, the army moved in and a hastily-built network of coastal fortifications and minefields was installed. As part of this, the order came to evacuate, at very short notice, the entire civil population of Shingle Street, seven miles north of Bawdsey, on 22 June – before the key events which would later fuel the German invasion legend are alleged to have taken place.

Residents were given just three days to find alternative accommodation, most moving inland to Hollesley and Alderton. 'With just one lorry to assist in the hasty exodus, villagers were able to remove only bare essentials … many larger chattels, such as furniture, had to be left behind,' wrote Essex author James Hayward in *The Bodies on the Beach*, his illuminating account of Shingle Street's much-debated wartime story, first published in 2001 by Norfolk firm CD41 Publishing. 'Sadly,' he added, 'over the next few months extensive looting took place.'[3]

While no doubt deeply distressing for those concerned, the haste was understandable. Invasion might come at any moment. The English coastline, indeed the nation itself, was highly vulnerable to attack. The priority had to be its defence, no matter what sacrifices were required in order to achieve this. There could be no certainty about the precise location for the feared German assault.

As it was, Hitler's *Unternehmen Seelöwe* (Operation Sea Lion), the plan for invading England, was beset by inter-service squabbles and considerable high-level doubt as to its chances of success. The plan had undergone many changes since it was first considered at the end of 1939. Certainly, the German Army did envisage at one stage an assault across the North Sea from the Low Countries against targeted beaches between The Wash and the River Thames. Conventional history, of course, tells us that this option, along with several others, was abandoned and the finalised scheme for invasion was concentrated on a cross-Channel attack on the English southeast from northern France – before the whole idea was scrapped altogether. Shingle Street's legend, however, adopts a wholly different slant to the accepted wisdom.

In the years that followed the conflict, the precise nature of the Suffolk hamlet's wartime involvement was a matter for earnest conjecture and speculation, aided by a complete lack of official explanation. The answers to the conundrum, it was widely believed, lay among the nation's archives at Kew, in a bundle of documents from the erstwhile Ministry of Home Security, set up in 1939 to oversee Britain's wartime civil defence. The papers were archived under the file reference HO 207/1175. However, that file had been locked away as an official secret, out of the reach of public scrutiny, until 2021. 'For decades this inexplicable secrecy boggled minds across East Anglia,' wrote James Hayward, a noted buster of wartime myths, in his 2001 book. 'It was all to do with a secret bomb, some hinted. Others found room for the Ultra secret.'

As the rumour mill relentlessly churned, many of the circulating stories centred on grim references to the discovery of charred bodies washed up in substantial numbers on the shore. Were these, as most of the rumours insisted, German? Had they been victims of a doomed attempt to invade Britain via a North Sea crossing from occupied territory and the English East Coast?

In 1992, the speculation reached an astonishing crescendo, ignited by an article in the 7 March edition of the Ipswich-based *East Anglian Daily Times*. This offered a wholly new twist on the legendary tale's usual definition of those who died. Eye-catchingly headlined, 'Dozens of soldiers killed in Nazi invasion blunder' the exclusive story merited its front page status, dramatically reporting a claim that 'dozens of *British* soldiers were burnt to death by one of their own men in a wartime exercise which went wrong'. Quoting 'new information' on the 1940 invasion rumour, the newspaper told readers that the incident allegedly had occurred 'during a training exercise near the radar installation at Bawdsey, just south of Shingle Street'.

The report explained that:

'part of the base's defences was a system known as PLUTO (Pipe Line Under The Ocean) in which drums of petrol were chained to concrete blocks under the sea and wired to detonators. In case of an enemy assault from the sea the drums would be blown and the petrol would rise to the surface where it could be set alight using tracer rounds.'

However, added the *EADT*, disaster had followed when the army decided to carry out a mock assault on Bawdsey. Naturally, they had contacted the radar station to say this would be taking place:

'but somehow the message was not passed on. Later that night, a sentry saw rubber dinghies approaching the base and, assuming it was the enemy, detonated the charges. The petrol was set alight by the tracer bullets from a machine gun post. Many soldiers died in the inferno and their bodies were carried out on the tide, only to be washed up on Shingle Street.'

There was a clear factual error in *EADT* journalist Henry Creagh's article. Operation PLUTO, the means by which oil was pumped through undersea pipelines to fuel the Allied advance from the Normandy beaches after D-Day in 1944 – running initially from Sandown Bay on the Isle of Wight coast to a point near Cherbourg and, later, across the much narrower stretch of sea between Dungeness, Kent, and Boulogne – was quite distinct from the fearsome-sounding device he was describing, a mistake that was quickly pointed out to him. Nonetheless, this was an intriguing slant on the invasion legend. Could the much-rumoured mass of German bodies washed up on

Shingle Street's beach in 1940 actually have been those of British soldiers tragically killed by a wickedly ingenious secret weapon turned on them by a compatriot in the mistaken belief they were the enemy – had it been a friendly fire disaster?

Among those interviewed by Creagh for his dramatic report was Ron Harris, one of the few local residents to remain in Shingle Street following its sudden evacuation. He had worked there during the war as a coastguard and remembered being given instructions to look for charred bodies. However, he could recall neither the date of the apparent tragedy nor any incident in which the sea had been set on fire. As for Creagh's actual source for the story, all *he* would say when questioned was that it had been 'a man close to the Ministry of Defence who had come across the classified papers [presumably those in file HO 207/1175] by chance'.

'It would be true to say that the story opened a Pandora's Box of theories and heated discussion,' wrote prolific Suffolk author Peter Haining in *Where the Eagle Landed*, a 2004 take for Robson Books on the county's vexed invasion legend.[4] In typically journalistic style, his book provided ample illustration of the near feverish interest prompted by Creagh's article. 'In general the responses were split between those who believed it was German invaders who had been burned alive and those who thought the victims were British troops killed in an accident,' added Haining. To complicate matters, some thought the casualties might have been Germans *dressed* as British troops. Others, preferring the theory of 'home-grown' disaster, suggested the drama had been the outcome of trials with chemical weapons.

Commissioned to drive for the War Department at the outbreak of hostilities, Arthur Smith told the *EADT* how he had been ordered in October 1940 to deliver eight tons of sand to 'a training area' on the coast – Shingle Street. He remembered it had looked 'just like a ghost town' when he got there. He had been advised that, on approaching the hamlet, a warden would tell him precisely where to unload the sand, 'and then I was to come straight back the way I came.'

The un-named official had some alarming news. Added Mr Smith:

'I'd heard Germans had tried to land, but the warden said, "I never saw any Germans but I know British soldiers were killed. They were a terrible sight and the flesh was burnt off their bones." He told me there had been no end of experiments, and this was one that went wrong – but was quickly covered up. He even pointed to a spot where one soldier had been found on the ground near to where I had to unload the sand. He then helped me to shovel the sand out of the lorry before I drove away.'

Arthur Smith was clearly an adherent of the chemical trials theory – and provided the *EADT* with some apparently graphic evidence:

'I believe the sand was to be used to douse a chemical experiment on the site that had gone terribly wrong. No one knew how many soldiers had been killed but the whole operation … was covered up. Later I made other trips to Shingle Street to collect shingle for coastal gun emplacements. I think I may have collected contaminated materials because a few weeks later two huge holes formed on the back of my neck. None of the doctors or nurses knew how they came about and they've left me scarred for life.'

It is probably an understatement to say that Henry Creagh had stirred up the proverbial hornets' nest with his article. His story continued to cause a great deal of excitable debate. Gripping tales, both first-hand from wartime veterans and those handed down through generations, followed. Details and likely dates for what correspondents were sure had been a hushed-up incident varied markedly, strung together by the core theme of bodies recovered in vast numbers from the beach, victims of sinister British ingenuity in the face of the invasion scare.

'The result was the kind of undignified media scramble spurred by *The Hitler Diaries*,' wrote James Hayward in an online summary for the BBC of his 2001 book. evoking memories of the international storm created by the 1993 publication in the West German magazine *Stern* of what purported to be extracts from the diaries of Adolf Hitler but were later exposed as fakes.

Reaction to Creagh's extraordinary Suffolk scoop, added Hayward, involved 'public outcry, the tabling of questions in the House of Commons, and the early declassification of HO 207/1175.' The file's release to the public in July 1992 in particular owed much to the prompting of the *East Anglian Daily Times* and the cross-party intervention of two local MPs, the Conservatives' John Gummer (Suffolk Coastal) and Labour's Jamie Cann (Ipswich), who successfully raised the matter with the then Tory Home Secretary, Ken Clarke. In the light of what transpired, they would have been forgiven for wondering whether it had been worth the effort!

James Hayward's compelling account of the saga noted that the hitherto secret and much anticipated dossier archived at Kew, headed *Evacuation of civil population from the village of Shingle Street in East Suffolk*, 'went some way towards proving that the reality of Shingle Street's wartime past was rather more prosaic.' No doubt to the disappointment of a great many invasion theorists, the Home Office file revealed nothing to confirm or reinforce the rumours of an enemy landing, let alone one in which the attacking force was burned to death. Neither was there anything in it to lend weight to the counter theory of a friendly fire disaster.

Sensational it most certainly was not! 'Inside were a total of 130 letters between the War Department, the Ministry of Home Security, government and army officials, civil servants, landowners and a number of residents of Shingle Street,' wrote Peter Haining in his entertaining book. 'The "top secret" information told of the measures taken to requisition all the dwellings in the hamlet in order that it could be used as a minefield and for testing new weapons.'

A passing reference in the file to the apparent testing of mustard gas at Shingle Street in April 1943 offered some scope for wishful thinking on the part of the more excitable among those convinced of a cover-up – but within days, there was official denial that this had ever taken place.

It came in a statement on 18 July from the Ministry of Defence, prompted by widespread public reluctance to accept that the newly-released file had not been strategically redacted to remove any references to the perceived wisdom of a thwarted German invasion and badly charred bodies on the beach. The MoD had been engaging in research of its own, delving through the available wartime records of both military and scientific activity on the Suffolk coast.

Not only did the MoD contradict the Home Office file by insisting there had been no trials at Shingle Street with mustard gas, its statement also effectively rubbished the stories of 'burning seas' with a categorical denial that any flame defence trials had been held there either (though such experiments were certainly carried out elsewhere on England's east coast – see below). Neither, the MoD asserted, was there any evidence in the military records to reinforce the claims that many lives had been lost in a training accident of any kind. As for German bodies strewn on the beach, the ministry had found records of just one German national washed up on the local shores. Indeed, there was 'no record of a large number of bodies being recovered from the beaches in the area in the summer, autumn or winter of 1940. It is believed this theory emanated from the erroneous reports that flame defences were used.'

While Shingle Street had been specifically mentioned in records of a 'paper exercise' by the British Army in July 1940 centred on an *imagined* enemy invasion, the ministry added that there was 'no evidence to support claims that British troops dressed in German uniform landed at Shingle Street during a mock invasion'. The legends, it appeared, were falling like ninepins. Could the MoD offer *any* solace to the committed conspiracy theorists? It seemed not.

The final part of its statement was especially significant, and not merely in terms of the Shingle Street legend. It stood then and, as this book was nearing its completion in 2016, it remained the contention and official stance of the MoD, and the British Government as a whole, on *all* the many rumours of seaborne attacks on the UK coast by German servicemen during the Second World War – and in that category we must include the rumoured raid on the Isle of Wight.

The MoD's concluding paragraph read:

'Equally, there is no evidence of any German invasion attempt or even German commando-style raids by sea or air. Indeed, there is no evidence in either the most highly classified contemporary British records, or apparently in the contemporary German records, of an actual attempt by the Germans to land in Britain, apart from the Channel Islands, which were occupied by the Germans after the fall of France.'

It could hardly have been clearer. Yet it did little, if anything, to quell the rumours. There remains a persistent belief among many people that the British authorities are refusing to come clean, determined to hide the truth of an attempted German landing at Shingle Street or, if not there, somewhere else on the shores of England. For the purposes of the present work, it is difficult not to conjecture about the Ministry of Defence's specific mention of a 'commando-style raid', albeit one that manifestly was intended to rule out that possibility for good.

It would be useful, perhaps, to rule out conclusively the Suffolk saga in order to 'clear the decks' as quickly as possible for an in-depth examination of the Isle of Wight legend. This, however, is simply not possible. The investigative waters of the latter are muddied by the complexities of the former. Separation is essential. We need to look more closely at Shingle Street in order to eliminate the possibility that conflation is a factor in the story of the island raid.

Legends will almost always emerge from a truth. As noted by the MoD in 1992, it is a verifiable fact that the body of a dead German *was* retrieved from the sea at Shingle Street, in the final week of October 1940. A further two were found at Bawdsey. However, the trio were airmen, killed when their Heinkel He-111 crashed into the North Sea almost a month earlier. The body of a fourth member of the bomber's crew was discovered nearly twenty miles further north at Aldeburgh. 'This sad quartet, the only Germans officially acknowledged as having landed near Shingle Street during the Second World War, were buried in Ipswich,' James Hayward recorded. 'Given the heightened tension of 1940, their numbers were no doubt exaggerated and played a part in establishing the Shingle Street myth.'

But there is more to the 'bodies on the beach' legend than this. The oft-repeated claim of a raiding force's demise by burning was rooted, though massively twisted, in a further grain of truth. Hitler, on 17 September, may have postponed indefinitely the planned German invasion of Britain but he had not, of course, notified the British whose home-based forces remained on constant invasion alert. James Hayward draws attention to a scheme to produce 'an impenetrable barrage of flame on the sea to prevent or destroy enemy ships attempting a landing' and records that the area's military command apparently suggested ideal sites for such barrages – essentially created by igniting oil on the water's surface – at offshore locations between Bawdsey and Felixstowe in the south-eastern corner of Suffolk's North Sea coast.

Though it had its drawbacks – high dependence on weather and sea conditions, for one thing, plus the distinct possibility that, in creating a voluminous smoke screen, it might actually aid the advance of an approaching seaborne enemy force – the idea of a flame barrage deterrent was certainly under discussion in Britain at the height of the 1940 invasion scare. Under the auspices of the remarkable Petroleum Warfare Department, trials would be held as the year progressed. Whether or not the four sites off the Suffolk coastline were ever seriously considered is a moot point. In the event, flame barrage demonstrations off the English east coast were actually held no further north than Shoeburyness, at the mouth of the Thames in Essex.

Yet the actuality of flame barrage development was, at the least, matched by the potential value the new defence measure's *rumoured* effectiveness could bring to the tide of international opinion – especially in the still neutral USA. The very idea that Britain possessed the ability to set the sea alight at will was a powerful weapon in itself, an eye-catching indication that the island nation, although seemingly at the mercy of Germany's all-conquering *blitzkrieg* offensive, was very far from beaten and perfectly able to strike back with terrifying weaponry at the enemy. Rumours, deliberately fanned from Britain. of an already tried and tested flame barrage filtered out of the country before any serious trials had taken place and spread across Europe like the wildfire promised by the sinister deterrent itself.

Compellingly, James Hayward asserts that the apparent suggestion of flame barrages off the four Suffolk beaches was a key part of the 'highly successful black propaganda exercise' coordinated by MI6, the Special Operations Executive (SOE) and the Directorate of Military Intelligence, a highly sophisticated bluff that had quickly become common knowledge abroad. Interest on the European continent intensified considerably when the barrage rumours acquired the darkly sensational embellishment that would later characterise Shingle Street's legend.

In the middle of September 1940 came the first rumours that German servicemen had been burnt – in many cases, fatally – by ingeniously ignited oil on the sea during an attempted landing on the British coast. The story was picked up by the American press in neutral Switzerland and given real credence by a US journalist's subsequent reports from Berlin of 'the longest Red Cross train I've ever seen' carrying what he had been told were victims of burns.

That the British did fan the flames of 'burning seas' propaganda in 1940 is confirmed by Winston Churchill himself, although the Suffolk coast did not feature at all in his account. As part of his epic history of the Second World War, which appeared as a six-volume series when first published by Houghton Mifflin in the USA between 1948 and 1953, Churchill dealt with the episode in the course of recalling the overall story of 1940's dramatic events in *Their Finest Hour*, the second volume in the series, published in 1949.[5] He was, of course, in a unique position to tell the story of the war, at least from the British perspective, but he was nonetheless restricted in what he was actually able to write. Revealing official wartime secrets – still sensitive issues such as the work carried out by Bletchley Park's code-breakers, for example – was out of the question, expressly forbidden under the terms of an agreement with Clement Attlee's post-war Labour government which otherwise allowed Churchill's research team generous access to, and use of, official papers to augment the former PM's own records, his comprehensive collection of 'personal minutes' compiled during his years in office.

Churchill obviously knew a lot more than he was able to reveal in his six books and, since these largely represented his individual perspective on the war, what he left out would also have included the omission from the narrative of matters he personally did not wish to record for posterity. While his researchers did a great deal of the preparatory work, Churchill remained the sole author. It was his name on the cover, his story, his version of events.

In the wider context of essential wartime (and post-war) 'news management' this is clearly something that is worth bearing in mind. It is unlikely, however, that confirming the 'burning seas' episode in print would have presented Churchill with a dilemma. If we accept – and this is certainly the view of most objective commentators today – that his account was a true reflection of the facts, he would no doubt have been more than pleased to relate it. 'War is a game that is played with a smile. If you can't smile, grin. If you can't grin, keep out of the way till you can!' he had advised an audience in October 1941. It is not hard to imagine him recalling these words when, surely with at least the hint of a grin, he sat down to write about the affair.

He recounted that, during August 1940,

'the corpses of about forty German soldiers were washed up at scattered points along the coast between the Isle of Wight and Cornwall. The Germans had been practising embarkations in the barges along the French coast. Some of these barges put out to sea in order to escape British bombing and were sunk either by bombing or bad weather. This was the source of a widespread rumour that the Germans had attempted an invasion and had suffered very heavy losses, either by drowning or by being burnt in patches of sea covered in flaming oil. We took no steps to contradict such tales, which spread freely through the occupied countries in wildly exaggerated form ...'

This was hardly a revelation. In 1946, three years before the publication of *Their Finest Hour*, Sir Donald Banks, Director-General of the Petroleum Warfare Department between 1940 and 1945, had described in his own book, *Flame over Britain*, how the trials and demonstrations of flame barrages failed to convince the military high command of the deterrent's likely effectiveness against an enemy force. As a result, the barrages were never developed to the point of actual deployment. Propaganda had always been seen as the real weapon. In his definitive work, published in London by Sampson Low, Marston & Co. and sub-titled *A Personal Narrative of Petroleum Warfare*, Sir Donald had written that:

'perhaps the greatest contribution from all [the PWD's] variegated efforts was in building up the great propaganda story of the flame defence of Britain which swept the continent of Europe in 1940.'

James Hayward's view is that stories of such dramatic events helped to keep the Americans on-side and willing eventually to provide vital war resources to Britain through lend–lease agreement – as actually happened in March 1941 with the passing of a bill in Washington that saw the USA supply aid to Britain, Free France and China, later extended to include the USSR.

On 25 September 1940, coinciding precisely with announcement of the British war planners' apparent preparedness for flame barrages off the Suffolk coast, the Nazi high command in Berlin felt compelled to use the international press to dismiss the, by now widely circulating, stories of 'many thousands of bodies of German soldiers … being washed ashore along the English Channel' as 'an indication of a situation that compels the British to put out such silly lies.'

Estimates of the German death toll varied considerably – as high as 80,000 in some of the more fanciful interpretations – but the figure most frequently quoted, thanks in no small measure to information distributed widely by the Free French at the behest of the British Ministry of Information, and via leaflets dropped liberally in Europe by the RAF, was around 30,000.

Inevitably, the 'burning sea' rumour bounced back to Britain and official suppression was equally inevitable. 'In the whole course of the war there was no story which gave me so much trouble as this one of the attempted German invasion, flaming oil on the water and 30,000 burned Germans,' the UK's chief press censor, Rear Admiral George Pirie Thomson, would later recall. Despite the official wartime censorship, the sensational story would continue to excite historical theorists in Britain, as well as the nation's media, for several decades to come.

Initial impressions in 1940 aside, it was not the English Channel, or at least somewhere along the English south coast, but Suffolk, and Shingle Street in particular, which became the persistent focus for many, though not all, of the post-war 'burning sea' rumours. The village's wartime evacuation and the recovery from the nearby sea of the dead German airmen were obvious factors. Another was the established secretive nature of activity in the area.

Whether or not this extended to wartime trials with chemical weapons, and precisely when this occurred, is still argued over today, despite the official denial from the Ministry of Defence in 1992. James Hayward's scepticism for the legends of war is well-known but, in depicting the demise of the hamlet's Lifeboat Inn – in explosive fashion – during September 1942, he does lend some persuasive literary weight to Shingle Street's rumoured association with chemical trials. However, his account equally serves as a knock-back for the theory that experiments with chemical weaponry were linked to an attempted German invasion and leaves no room for any suggestion that the loss of the inn itself can similarly be ascribed to the enemy.

'The Chemical Defence Research Establishment at Porton Down [Wiltshire] was casting around for land and buildings on which to test a new device. The device was an experimental 250lb bomb which combined liquid mustard with high explosive. The scientists were offered the use of deserted Shingle Street. Preceded by several dry runs, their bomb was dropped there from the air on 28 March 1943. It scored a direct hit on the Lifeboat Inn.'

Secretive Shingle Street thus possessed all the ingredients for an irresistible cocktail of mystery and intrigue, the ideal location, or so it seemed, for the greatest British cover-up of the war. In 2002, a year after publication of James Hayward's book, the debate was reignited by a claim made on regional BBC television that the 'burning bodies' invasion story had been faked to boost British morale, a twist on Hayward's version of events. The essence of BBC East's *Inside Out* programme suggested that German-born journalist Sefton Delmer, who lived in Suffolk and had been recruited by the UK's Political Warfare Executive to mastermind the nation's 'black propaganda' broadcasts, had concocted the story himself in 1940.

A British national despite his 1904 birth (to Australian parents) in Berlin, Delmer was a man with a fascinating life story. His family had been repatriated to the UK in 1917 through a prisoner exchange between the German and British governments. Initially educated at St Paul's School, London, Delmer studied modern languages at Oxford University before beginning a distinguished career in journalism which saw him return to Germany as the head of the *Daily Express's* Berlin bureau. While there he became the first British journalist to interview Adolf Hitler. Transferring to the newspaper's Paris bureau in 1933, he reported extensively on major events before and during the first months of the Second World War before his recruitment in September 1940 to the new propaganda role with the PWE in Britain. This involvement in the black arts of psychological warfare suited him.

Respected investigative journalist Phillip Knightley told the BBC:

'I would not put it past Sefton Delmer to deliberately ignite a few hundred gallons of petrol somewhere off the coast where he knew it would be seen, and to make certain some of the bodies that came ashore had signs of burning.'[6, 7]

And, if bodies *had* been washed ashore at Shingle Street, the programme went on to claim, they could actually have been the remains of men whose lives were among those lost on a British naval destroyer attacked by the enemy. Creating the impression that they were part of a German raiding party would have served to cover up the truth.

As reinforcement for Knightley's theory, *Inside Out* included a contribution from Thomas Waterhouse who told how in 1940 he was serving with a Royal Navy destroyer flotilla alerted to a reported sighting of enemy invasion barges off the coast of Nazi-occupied Denmark. One destroyer was sunk in a minefield, he told the programme.

'We were unable to know what happened to our casualties but it would be quite believable that for local consumption people had said they were the results of a failed invasion attempt. People didn't want bad news and they were prepared to go along with any cock and bull story to keep their spirits up.'

Unsurprisingly, this was picked up by the regional press. The *Ipswich Star* ran it prominently, quite properly seeking to balance the claim by speaking with Ronald Ashford, an 81-year-old retired jeweller in Aldeburgh who remained convinced the Germans *had* tried to invade Suffolk in August 1940. A Home Guardsman at the time, he was positioned one evening at the 'lower end' of Aldeburgh, to the north of Shingle Street, when a red alert was passed to his unit. They heard 'tremendous gunfire and explosions,' he said, and were told a German landing had taken place. Eyewitnesses, he added, said the shoreline was 'littered with burned bodies.'

A prominent proponent of the Suffolk invasion story, Ron Ashford had set up a website in support of his beliefs. He claimed to the *Ipswich Star* that the German target was the radar station at Bawdsey and suggested that the would-be raiding force had also intended to capture the nearby airfield at RAF Martlesham Heath. He had no time for the 'black propaganda' theory. 'I was not there but near enough to see what went on. I am a living witness to what happened and these are not lies that I have written about and researched,' he told the Ipswich paper.

Ron Ashford's recall of those seemingly dramatic events in August 1940 could not justifiably be airily dismissed as time-worn fantasy. Consistently sincere and erudite in making his case when the media sought him out, as they often did, he was a convincing advocate, a man whose story many wanted to believe, dismissing the possibility – and rightly so – that he was making the whole thing up. In June 2010, he was again an obvious source for comment when the *Eastern Daily Press* posed the question – 'could the county's [Suffolk's] rapidly eroding shoreline provide answers to what really happened at Shingle Street ... one August night in 1940?'

The *EDP* described how local man Graham Newman, who regularly walked his dog on the beach close to his home at Bawdsey, had over the years discovered 'a number of pieces of what look like molten metal ... however, he has recently become concerned at the rate the beach is eroding and is now looking for answers as to where these items may have come from.'

Mr Newman, aged sixty-eight, who had served in the Royal Navy and had also worked as a coastguard, was quoted as saying that:

> '... with the shifting shingle caused by the action of the tide, the profile of the beach at Bawdsey changes. A couple of times a year, at unpredictable times and tides, a large stretch of black, charred beach is revealed. On close inspection of this area, I have found many items of melted iron. These are generally just "blobs" but I have found half-melted tools and pieces with what appear to be rivet holes in them. This area is soon re-covered by sand until the sea decides to reveal these phenomena again. I just think it's very interesting and I'd like to know where they came from or what caused this.'

He wondered whether the mysterious metal objects were from an old ship but put forward another possibility. 'Could it be evidence of the German invasion at Shingle Street?'

In reviewing the legend, the newspaper reported the claims that:

'a flotilla of small vessels commandeered by the German army set out across the North Sea and landed at Shingle Street. British forces had previously covertly added fortifications to selected parts of the East Anglian coast – laying a series of pipelines in the sea, just past the low tide line. When the time came these pipelines were pumped full of a flammable liquid and the sea "set alight." Many of the boats nearest to the shore are said to have been caught in the blaze, resulting in German casualties. In the aftermath of the attack there were unconfirmed reports of many burned bodies littering the shoreline from Shingle Street to Harwich.'

Ron Ashcroft had his cue and he did not disappoint:

'We saw the sky light up and the sound of gunfire and explosions. It went on until six in the morning. We *knew* it took place. Speculation and controversy still exist as to the events stated, but I am positive that in time they will be proven.'

Also in 2010, the former Aldeburgh Home Guardsman's relentless campaign for official confirmation of what he was absolutely certain was the truth about Shingle Street gained a nationwide audience when his story was featured on the Discovery History TV channel as part of its *Wartime Secrets with Harry Harris* series. London taxi driver and history guide, the genial Harris spoke at length with Ron Ashcroft, clearly captivated by the sheer force and detail of what he was being told about 'how close we came to being invaded in the summer of 1940'.

Harris's interviewee stuck to his well-rehearsed story. From Aldeburgh he, and those with him, suddenly had 'seen the sea setting on fire and a big orange glow. Then, shortly after that, there were explosions and gunfire that went on all night. The rumour was that there was an invasion taking place … we were told to watch for paratroopers, which we hadn't been told previously.' This was an interesting point. It was widely believed in 1940 that the arrival of German paratroops would presage a full-scale seaborne invasion. Here, the clear implication from Ron Ashford was that the seaborne invaders had reached English shores in advance of the airborne troops. Not that it had done them much good. 'It appears the invasion failed because we'd set up an oil pipeline along the seashore and set the sea on fire,' explained the veteran.

'The Germans were caught, not expecting this, which meant that many of their boats and their men were badly burnt and some of the ships were destroyed. In the morning a lot of bodies were picked up along the shoreline. We were told afterwards that there were three burial pits and that's where they were put.'

This was one of Ron Ashford's more expansive accounts of the Shingle Street mystery but, while clearly in awe, Harry Harris posed a key question.

'Did you get down to the beach to see the bodies come up?' he asked. The former Home Guardsman had to admit he hadn't actually seen any bodies on the beach – but there was a good reason for that. The beach at Shingle Street was a restricted area; no one was allowed there.

Despite this, he was convinced the beach was littered with dead Germans who had travelled across the North Sea in a large armada. 'There must have been three or four thousand trying to invade this coast and they were actually fighting on English soil for about nine hours,' he said, a remark guaranteed to wow the presenter and the TV audience – and no doubt those who have since watched the many repeats of this remarkable interview. Harry was impressed: 'So you had a battle going on here on the coast in Suffolk – the Germans really did land here!'

'Yes, they did land – lots of them,' replied Ron, agreeing with the presenter that this extraordinarily dramatic episode had subsequently been wiped from the British nation's war record. 'Yes, it was all covered up … it would have been news [the authorities] didn't want brought out so they hushed it up. It's not supposed to come out [into the public record] until 2021.'

This was a clear reference to the documents archived together in Home Office file HO 207/1175. Maybe Ron Ashford was unaware of the file's declassification twenty-eight years early in 1993 and of its total lack of supporting evidence for his dramatic claims. Learning subsequently of its early release, Harry Harris was naturally anxious to see the file. Accompanied for expert guidance by Dr Harry Bennett, Associate Professor (Reader) in History at Plymouth University, he was filmed visiting the National Archives at Kew in order to examine its content. 'So what was it that they were trying to keep hidden from us?' he asked.

Dr Bennett agreed the original 2021 'closed' date would immediately have provoked suspicions of a hidden State secret. 'But when we begin to get into the file we start to notice that it's much more mundane,' he said, selecting a typical document from the file which more than made his point – a letter from the War Department's land agent to a Shingle Street resident confirming that compensation would be paid following a break-in at his property by soldiers during the wartime military occupation of the hamlet. No mention of bodies on the beach.

Dr Bennett told the clearly disappointed television presenter:

'It's about properties … broken glass … missing roof tiles … somebody's kicked in my front door! One of the reasons this file was closed [classified] was because this is, in effect, data protection. It's about not exposing people to any sort of comeback. The letter was sent to someone asking the government for money. But there was a war on. In effect they were saying, "what kind of person are you!" As simple as that. That's the secret – there was *no* secret!'

Once more the Shingle Street legend had been undermined by the official evidence – or the lack of it. Harry Harris was understandably perplexed. His words to Dr Bennett probably echoed the thoughts of a good many, if not most, of his TV audience. 'I do still believe that what Ron saw was, for him, real and I am not going to dismiss what he told me,' he said. Turning to his expert guest, he added, 'but what you are saying is that there was no official cover-up?'

This was a low point for the Suffolk invasion legend as Dr Bennett replied:

'There was *no* official cover-up. For the conspiracy theories to work, we have to accept that all of the British records have been doctored, and all the German records, too. What we are left with when we begin properly to evaluate the story isn't that extensive because, let's turn the tables for a minute, what evidence have *you* got to suggest that a landing took place at Shingle Street?'

Harry was not beaten yet, Ron Ashford's bulging file of apparently corroborative witness evidence clearly still fresh in his mind as he responded:

'The only evidence I've got are Ron's letters from other people saying "it wasn't only you, Ron – my father witnessed this, my grandfather witnessed that." It all seemed pretty convincing to me.'

It was a perfectly fair point for the presenter to make, but Dr Bennett replied:

'I have no doubt at all in terms of what people heard and what people saw. The question is, what story you build on top of this evidence. There's a war on. Bodies are washing up on beaches all over the place, especially after Dunkirk. You have coastal gunners who have itchy trigger fingers. They start shooting and somebody at the next post thinks, "I'd better join in, just in case." So you've got the appearance of an enormous firefight taking place. Does it substantiate the idea of a German invasion? Well, no it doesn't – nowhere near.'

Harry Harris had one more throw of the dice. He had heard from people who told of church bells, normally silent during wartime, being rung – the official signal of enemy invasion. Dr Bennett had an answer to that, too.

'The code word *Cromwell* is used by the Chiefs of Staff to say that an invasion appears imminent. They're not saying it's definite but some people on the ground – jumpy, nervous, tense – are saying, "hang on a minute, imminent means that's in the next twenty-four hours," and the alarm is sounded. There were one or two instances where bridges were actually blown because they thought the German paratroopers were about to land.'

It is well documented that the *Cromwell* signal was issued by the War Office on 7 September 1940, instructing all home defence forces in the UK to adopt 'the highest degree of readiness' in preparation for an expected German invasion 'at any time.' Weather and tidal conditions were particularly favourable for an enemy assault but the alert was soon cancelled as a false alarm

The TV programme's presenter could only respond to Dr Bennett's clinically thorough deflation of the Suffolk invasion legend by concluding that 'the debate rages on'. He was right, but Ron Ashford's leading role in the story would soon be over. He died at Aldeburgh at the age of ninety-one in December 2013. The legend, however, was destined to outlive him.

As recently as October 2014, the Shingle Street story was once again enthralling a TV audience when it was featured in the BBC's magazine-style programme, *The One Show*. In essence there was little that was new about the content. Gravely, presenter Gyles Brandreth outlined how 'invasion was repelled in a particularly gruesome fashion – the enemy was burnt alive by a wall of flame rising from the sea and the shingle was littered with charred bodies.'

Relatives of former Royal Engineers 2nd Lieutenant Sonny Ambrose, who years earlier had spoken of what had proved a life-changing experience at Shingle Street in August 1940, explained that, according to his story, 'when the tide was low they put pipes out on the sand, or in the sand, and filled them with petrol.' The ex-soldier had claimed he was told 'the Germans were coming.' He said 'they had to set fire to the water … it gave him nightmares all the time because he could hear the screaming and yelling of those who were getting burnt alive.'

Ambrose's sister-in-law was asked by Brandreth if her husband had spoken of the change he had seen in his brother following this apparently horrifying episode. 'Oh yes,' she replied, 'as a young man he [Sonny] was so full of life – he enjoyed life so much. He changed completely.'

The point was made by *The One Show* that there were now no surviving first-hand witnesses to the alleged incident, 'but testimony remains from many of them,' added Brandreth as quotes from the regional press were flashed on the screen recalling the words of relatives of others who claimed to have been there:

'He said he had picked up dead bodies – Germans' … 'the beach was covered by dozens of charred bodies – my grandfather was devastated by it all' … 'all these bodies were very badly burnt' … 'laying on the beach as far as the eye could see.'

Not exactly revelatory accounts, yet gripping nonetheless. 'But what's the truth?' asked Brandreth. 'Did the eagle really land here at Shingle Street? Did the sea really catch fire? The loss of soldiers, weaponry and equipment at Dunkirk meant other means of defence were needed.'

Enter myth-buster James Hayward. Introduced as an historian and expert on the wartime defence of the East Coast, Hayward was unequivocal. Retracing his well-worn path of inquiry, he told of the formation of Britain's Petroleum Warfare Department 'with the aim of using petroleum offensively against the enemy' and outlined the origin of the sea flame barrage. Newsreel footage was shown to prove that, however far-fetched, the technology did exist. 'From submarine pipelines, oil bubbles to the surface,' ran the soundtrack. 'As the dark patches merge together they are electrically ignited from the shore and the sea bursts into flames.'

But not, according to Hayward, at Shingle Street. 'There's no evidence … of charred bodies being washed up here and there never was a flame barrage set up anywhere in this location,' he said, patiently, one suspects, reiterating the conclusions in his book. 'A couple of German airmen [were] washed up on the beach and this may have been confused with the wider story of dozens, or hundreds, or even thousands, of German soldiers being washed up.' His explanation for the legendary Shingle Street rumours was, of course, the 'great propaganda campaign to spread these stories of flame barrages or invasions that had failed. We needed to convince America that we were still in the game and we were going to fight back against Hitler.'

Concluding the feature, Gyles Brandreth rightly noted that the Ministry of Defence continued to deny outright the failed Suffolk invasion ever took place, but he added that, 'for some local people it will be forever etched in their family history. This is a mystery that simply won't go away.'

There will probably always be adherents to the Shingle Street legend. It is too good a story to die. That said, the less than sensational contents of Home Office file HO 207/1175 and the persuasive counter-arguments of historical specialists James Hayward and Harry Bennett are impossible to dismiss. In his comprehensively researched book, *The Battle of the East Coast (1939–1945)*, which he self-published in 1994, Julian Foynes also concludes that the invasion legend is just that – a story lacking any reliable documentary evidence. As for Peter Haining, who died in 2007, while he was sure German servicemen *did* land on a Suffolk beach in the summer of 1940 – as his 2004 book set out to prove – he, too, was convinced it did not happen at Shingle Street and bore none of the characteristics of the 'bodies on the beach' rumour archive.

His version, that the crew of a solitary E-boat made landfall further north at Sizewell Gap on an apparently speculative mission, was markedly low-key compared with the Shingle Street stories – and arguably more believable as a result. His case was based largely on the recollections of a local man who, years after the war, claimed to have found recently discarded items of German origin, including chocolate, the remains of an apparent meal, cigarette ends and – regarded as the principal find – a naval officer's cap, on a beach he had visited as a teenager for a morning swim during the final weekend of July 1940. He had not reported the discovery to anyone at the time and had later sold the German cap at an auction. Haining's detractors regarded his 'hard evidence' as decidedly scanty although, as the author went to great lengths to demonstrate in his book, the records of E-boat activity off the East Coast in 1940 and other circumstantial evidence did at least add an air of plausibility to his tale.

In setting out the case which forms the basis for this current work, and distinguishing it from other stories of wartime German landings in Britain, it is perhaps helpful that, despite the fact the Isle of Wight does feature among the many other folktales of charred German bodies on English beaches, the island's tale of a commando-style assault in 1943 shares the distinction of the Suffolk incident described by Peter Haining in not being linked to flame barrages, friendly fire disasters or chemical weaponry catastrophes in any way, nor to a heavy loss of life, yet points to a considerably more significant landfall than that suggested in Mr Haining's book.

Among the tales that *do* link the island to a German invasion foiled by the flaming sea deterrent, some of the more prominent suggest a mass loss of enemy life on local shores in August 1942 rather than at any time in 1940. One version, first made public in September 2005 when it was featured on the BBC's *WW2 People's War* website, tells of the sea 'erupting in flames' close to The Needles, apparently in full view of those on board a Royal Navy patrol boat. According to one of them, former commando Ernest Brooks, around one thousand Germans had tried to invade via the waters south of the island. The suggestion here would appear to be that they had collectively fallen victim to the terrifying British flame barrage.

It seems the strength of this apparently doomed invasion force was calculated from the number of German vessels that had, according to the source of the story, left the Normandy port of Dieppe that morning, 10 August. On the previous day, aerial reconnaissance had shown a harbour full of boats. Photographs taken the following morning revealed they had virtually all departed. It was further implied that the Germans had employed 'huge rowing boats,' capable of transporting fifty men, as their landing craft. Fine detail, perhaps, but this story made little sense.

Dieppe was certainly at the heart of planning for a cross-Channel raid in August 1942 – but the other way round! Early on 19 August, just over a week after the supposedly foiled Isle of Wight invasion was said to have taken place, combined Allied ground forces, principally Canadian, with Royal Navy and RAF support, attacked the occupied French port in large numbers. The outcome has been closely chronicled. Dieppe was well defended. The enemy was ready and waiting. Some maintain today that the Germans had precise warning specific to Dieppe; others prefer the view that, while an attack was expected somewhere on the northern French coast, leading to general preparedness, the specific location for the raid was unknown until it happened. Whatever the truth of that, the raid on Dieppe was a catastrophe. The number of Allied losses – those killed, wounded or taken prisoner – was horrifically high.

The statistics make grim reading. The 5,000-strong Canadian force was decimated, with 3,367 killed, wounded or taken captive. Losses also included 275 of the one thousand British commandos who took part in the raid, code-named Operation Jubilee, while Royal Navy casualties numbered 550 killed or wounded (together with a destroyer and thirty-three landing craft). The RAF lost sixty-two men, with a further thirty wounded and seventeen taken prisoner. Eighty-four British Spitfire and Hurricane fighter planes were shot down, plus ten US Mustang P-51 fighters and six Douglas Boston bombers. The defending Germans fared far better but nonetheless suffered 311 fatalities, with a further two hundred wounded. The Luftwaffe lost forty-eight aircraft, a combination of Fw-190 fighters and Do-217 utility planes.

While German casualties were relatively light, some of Dieppe's defenders suffered horribly. Taken prisoner, they drowned in the confused wake of the Canadian withdrawal. The bodies of these men *were* washed ashore, though still on the French coast. When they were found by their compatriots it was discovered they had been shackled. Orders captured from the raiding force appeared to show this had been deliberate Allied policy at Dieppe. There were unfortunate repercussions for prisoners of war on both sides of the divide. Hitler retaliated by ordering the shackling of Canadians in German captivity which, in turn, provoked Britain and a reluctant Canada to similarly restrict Germans held in Canadian PoW camps – a spiteful tit-for-tat that, rightly, soon petered out, though only after intervention by the International Red Cross.

The Germans emerged the victors at Dieppe but any suggestion that, days earlier, they had attempted a sizeable assault on the Isle of Wight is simply not credible. Hitler had long since abandoned any thoughts of invading England. The Luftwaffe had failed to gain the essential pre-requisite of aerial supremacy in 1940 when the war in the West was Hitler's prime concern. In August 1942 he was otherwise preoccupied – notably by the situation in the East as his forces strove once more to gain the upper hand in the ferocious war with the Soviet Union. An invasion of the Isle of Wight at that time was very far indeed from the Führer's mind.

A smaller scale commando-style raid on the island is a more realistic option for the origins of this particular tale, though there is no official record of this. However, its obvious links to flame barrages and possible confusion during the story's re-telling with confirmed historical events – the holding of a 'burning sea' demonstration on the northern shores of the Solent in 1940 and the Dieppe disaster two years later – point firmly to the conclusion that it is just a myth.

That Solent trial of the flame barrage, watched by a large crowd of invited spectators, took place on 24 August 1940 near the Hampshire village of Titchfield, which lies just over three miles from Fareham. Tanker wagons pumped oil down pipes running from the top of a thirty-foot (ten metre) high cliff into the sea. The fuel was ignited by flares and a combination of sodium and petrol pellets. In seconds a wall of flame was produced, causing the water to boil. While dramatic, the trial's success was somewhat offset by the improbably favourable conditions in the sheltered waters of the Solent, with a calm sun-warmed sea and only light winds. The possibility that the Hampshire demo, only a few miles from the Isle of Wight coast, helped to foster the legend of a failed German invasion via the island in 1942 seems likely

Interestingly, 1942 was also the backdrop for a similar story, circulated via the same BBC website in 2005, which suggested a mass loss of German life during an invasion attempt on the Dorset coast. Ernest (Jim) Buckland recalled:

'I was in the Royal Corps of Signals and was posted to the Chief Signal Officer's Staff in London. Each day we used to receive classified security reports of the German troop movements, aircraft losses and naval losses. In one of these reports we received information that trainloads of wounded German soldiers with horrific burns were going through Belgium, back to Germany. We later learned that there had been an attempted invasion on the Dorset coast, which had been beaten back by the use of FIDO [sic – the acronym is incorrectly used here], an oil system which sprayed the sea and was set on fire.'

In fact, FIDO had nothing to do with sprayed oil or burning seas. Instead, the acronym referred to the Fog Investigation and Dispersal Operation devised by British scientists as a means of dispensing fog (and dense smoke) from an airfield so that aircraft could land safely. Aside from this, there is no reason to doubt Jim Buckland's story. The information very probably *was* relayed to the signals officers in the way he described. Its basis, however, can be dismissed as apocryphal. In all respects, the message was typical of the 'official rumours' first heard in 1940. Donald Banks did include Studland Bay on Dorset's eastern coast among other sites on the south coast – in Kent and East Sussex – used for flame barrage experimentation by the Petroleum Warfare Department, but the rumoured invasion of the Dorset shores has 'myth' written all over it. This is not false testimony today, but it was back in 1942.

It is not hard today to come across Isle of Wight wartime stories which typify the 'burning seas' legend. Cecil Petty recalled receiving a letter from an uncle who served with the island's Home Guard and wrote that the Germans had tried to land on the beaches between Atherfield and Brook, on the south-western coast, 'but our troops had set fire to the sea and none of them had got ashore alive. "Don't talk about this" was his warning to me. I heard the same in the 1950s-60s from an old fisherman who lived near the old lifeboat station at Brook. I seem to recall he said something about Brook or Chale churchyards.' Suggestions that German victims of landings thwarted by a British sea-fire deterrent were hastily buried in mass graves at local churchyards or other convenient sites are a common feature of such tales.

In 2005, islander Rob Martin's research into the origins of the tales drew a similar response, with a Home Guardsman again at the centre of the story, when he appealed for information via an Isle of Wight history website. This particular tale, set in the island's north-eastern sector, illustrates the large, in relative terms, geographical spread of the many stories of this type.

The response came from local historian and author Andy Gilliam who vividly remembered his late mother talking about her father who was in the Home Guard.

'Apparently, one night his unit, presumably Ryde-based as he lived in the town, was, along with several others, called out. He didn't return until late the next day, exhausted, dirty and visibly shaken. He said that he was unable to discuss where he had been or what had happened. My mother said there was much talk of invasion around this time and that, although nothing was confirmed, it was generally implied that something out of the ordinary had definitely happened that night …'

Barbara Haden, of Carisbrooke, who has since died, often recounted a story told by her father. A prison officer at Parkhurst, he was a wartime member of the Auxiliary Units, the 'secret army' of civilians set up in the Isle of Wight and elsewhere along the British coast as a shadowy, well-drilled resistance force whose underground hideouts in the countryside, stocked with munitions and short-term survival rations, were excavated as bases for sabotage should the enemy succeed in invading the locality. According to this story, the Germans had attempted to do exactly that in 1940, but their seaborne assault on the island's south-western shoreline had been met with the ferocious flaming sea deterrent, fuelled, it was claimed, from a petrol pipeline laid across the western half of the isle. The charred bodies of the victims had been washed up at Compton Bay, northwest of Atherfield and Brook, and quickly interred nearby.

Gareth Sprack, from Ryde, offered perhaps the most circumspect of the Isle of Wight's catalogue of 'bodies on the beach' tales in recalling one of his father Peter's many stories of days with the wartime ARP (Air Raid Precautions) service on the island.

'One night, when my dad was not himself on duty, his colleagues from Shanklin, with another man from Sandown, had to go to Culver [towards the isle's eastern-most point] to pick up burnt German bodies on the beach at the foot of the cliffs. But, of course, with all the shipping that was being sunk at one point or other in the Channel and the aircraft that were being shot down, bodies were coming ashore all the time and, in terms of the enemy, virtually all of those were German airmen. This sort of thing quickly becomes the subject of Chinese whispers. The ARP guys pick up three bodies, a standard German aircrew, but by the time the story has gone through four other people in turn, the number quickly becomes thirty German bodies – and so it goes on.'

The essential lesson here is that, no matter how earnestly they are told, caution should always be exercised against easy acceptance as the truth of spectacularly dramatic, often horrific, but officially unsubstantiated, wartime tales such as those involving a foiled German invasion of the United Kingdom, and to take many, if not most, with the proverbial pinch of salt. There is no proof or hard indisputable evidence that Nazi Germany ever attempted to invade these islands. Again, it is perhaps useful in the context of the current work that the 1943 Isle of Wight legend does not suggest a German invasion but the far more probable commando-style raid.

That said, to pursue as probable fact a German raid on an island just a few miles adrift from England's south coast does, on the face of it, still invite a fair degree of scepticism and, the argument goes, if it really did take place, while it may well have been hushed up at the time for understandable reasons, it would surely have come to light by now, formally enshrined in official history. The vast majority of questionable Second World War tales can be, and have been, exposed as myths by a close study of archival records which have surfaced since the war's conclusion, long since freed of the need for secrecy, propaganda and the massaging of public morale. Yet the suggestion of a German raid on the Isle of Wight in 1943 cannot be summarily dismissed as fantasy. At the time of writing, there was no available British archival record to *prove* that it happened, but neither was there anything to say conclusively that it did not, and, as this book will make clear, there was powerful evidence elsewhere to support it. As with Shingle Street, it is a story which has run and run – but one that still has legs.

Chapter 2

Examination: 'one absolutely splendid raid'

M ost of what little has been written in this country about the possibility of a commando-style enemy raid during the Second World War in the south of England – as distinct from a full-scale attempt at invasion – stems from a few lines of text recorded in its journal by the Royal United Services Institute (RUSI) in 1947. It is a comment by the late Major-General Robert Laycock, a remark that is not just intriguing but, given his unquestionable status, highly compelling too.

Laycock had recently relinquished his key wartime role as Britain's Chief of Combined Operations, having taken over the job from the second appointee, Lord Louis Mountbatten, in 1943 when he was thirty-six years old. Earlier, he had served with British commando forces in North Africa, Crete, Sicily and Italy 'The commando-raider concept personified' said Vice-Admiral Sir Philip Vian by way of introduction when he chaired the Institute's 15 October 1947 meeting in London. Laycock spoke at length in detailing for his audience an overview of British commando raids carried out in the war and the lessons learned from them. His lecture and the questions which followed were recorded verbatim for the *RUSI Journal* and it was in answering the first question put to him that Laycock unhesitatingly made apparently revelatory remarks which to this day fuel speculation about a German landing in the United Kingdom.[1]

'I would like to ask the lecturer,' said Vice-Admiral Cecil Usborne, former Director of Naval Intelligence, 'if there are any examples of German raids which are at all comparable to our own?'

Laycock's reply, while offered in almost light-hearted vein, was effusive in evident admiration:

'There was one absolutely splendid raid carried out by the Germans from the Channel Islands which was almost one hundred per cent successful. As far as I know it is the only example of that type of raid. I can't think why the Germans did not try more, but it doesn't seem to have been in their normal idea of making war. This one was the only one of its kind I know of, and we were rather jealous of it; it went very well indeed. Of course, there were also the very small-scale raids carried out by the Italian saboteurs in the Mediterranean theatre, but they were nearly always rounded up before they had done much harm.'

Frustratingly, Laycock, who died in 1968 at the age of sixty, was not questioned further by the august gathering in London and made no other mention of the 'splendid' German raid at his RUSI lecture or, as far as is known, anywhere else, declining to reveal – though he surely must have known – the location, date, purpose and specific outcome of the enemy landing. We are left to conjecture, but his specific reference to the Channel Islands as launch-pad for the operation seems, at least on the surface, a tantalising piece of information which ties in neatly with one version of the Isle of Wight story and has added considerable weight to the tale.

Exactly sixty years later, writing in *Commando Country*, his comprehensive 2007 account of wartime training undertaken in the Scottish Highlands by special British forces, Dr Stuart Allan strayed southwards to add apparently authoritative endorsement of the story. A senior curator at National Museums Scotland, his book's publishers, Dr Allan noted that the episode described by Robert Laycock 'is believed to have been an attack against a radar station on the south coast of the Isle of Wight, launched from the occupied Channel Island of Alderney in 1941.' Despite the ill-fitting reference to 1941, two years earlier than the more favoured 1943 setting, it is indeed tempting to link Laycock's comment with the raid folklore which persists on the Isle of Wight. But, while that link cannot be discounted, an alternative possibility exists.

A propaganda coup for the all-conquering Third Reich at the expense of Britain, German occupation of the Channel Islands, demilitarised by the British as of little strategic relevance, began on 30 June 1940. Germany subsequently exercised unbroken control over the islands for the remainder of the war until the liberation of Jersey and Guernsey was finally achieved on 9 May 1945, with Sark freed the following day and German personnel on Alderney formally relinquishing control on the 16th – nearly a year after the D–Day invasion of the nearby Normandy beaches in June 1944 had set in train the removal of all occupying Nazi forces from western Europe, and several days after the final surrender of Germany had ended the European war.

Massively fortified during the occupation as part of Hitler's extensive Atlantic Wall of defence, the islands had been side-stepped by the Allies in the 1944 landings, but the invasion of Normandy had cut off the occupying garrison's vital French supply lines, leaving its beleaguered troops and the many residents still on the islands facing extreme hardship, starved of food and fuel, during the final year of war.

'Let 'em starve. No fighting. They can rot at their leisure,' was Winston Churchill's typically blunt response in September 1944 to the plight of the islands' German garrison. While this potentially meant that the islanders, at the mercy of their captors, would effectively be left to rot alongside them, Churchill had no intention of risking British forces in a strategically unnecessary assault against the enemy's powerful military presence in Jersey, Guernsey and the otherwise evacuated fortress island of Alderney. Protracted negotiations eventually saw the German authorities, reminded by the British of their obligation to feed and care for a civilian population under occupation, agree to the delivery of essential supplies for the islanders via a series of shipments organised by the Red Cross. The first arrived from Lisbon at the end of December 1944 aboard the SS *Vega*, a combination of food parcels, diet supplements for the sick, medical and surgical supplies, salt, soap, cigarettes and children's clothing.

The *Vega* would sail five more times with further supplies from the Red Cross up until the end of the war but, in the meantime, the Germans remained critically short of the commodities needed to sustain their presence. It was this desperate state of affairs which lay behind a decision to mount a daring raid from Jersey against the small French port of Granville, thirty nautical miles to the southeast, on 8–9 March 1945. It is right to add that sheer boredom was almost certainly a further motivating factor for an operation which, despite taking place at such an advanced stage in the war, allowed the stranded German armed forces – land, sea and air combined – one last defiant opportunity to do something to alleviate their military impotence and shattered morale.

The extraordinary events which precipitated the raid on the Allied-held Normandy port owed their origins to the existence at Granville of a US-run prisoner of war camp. During December 1944 five of its German inmates – four paratroopers and a naval cadet – escaped the poorly-guarded enclosure and later set sail for the Channel Islands in a stolen American landing craft (LCVP). Navigating with the aid of just a compass and a hand-drawn map, and surviving an attack by the Royal Navy en route, they made it as far as Les Minquiers, a group of islets and rocks nine miles to the south of Jersey where the Germans manned an observation post. Unsurprisingly mistaken for the enemy, they were initially fired upon but, with their true identity established, were then directed to the safety of the Jersey port of St Helier.

Once ashore, they were naturally given the warmest of receptions and treated as heroes by the occupying German forces, a rare highlight in a war of ever-increasing lows. The mood of the garrison, especially among the senior command, lifted still further when the escapees reported seeing several ships discharging coal in Granville harbour. Coal was a desperately needed commodity in the islands. Dockside warehouses appeared to offer the prospect of other much-needed supplies. Was this the chance to grab some from the enemy and restore a degree of purpose to what had become an otherwise pointless continued occupation? When the escapees were also able to outline to senior officers the disposition of US forces in the Granville area, the die was cast. Planning for a raid on the port began in earnest.

From the German perspective, the story was destined to turn bitter-sweet. News of the five ex-prisoners' heroics reached Hitler. The Führer summoned the men to Berlin so that he could personally decorate them for their daring. That was risky – shamefully so. The transport plane sent to pick them up never made it back to Germany, shot down by Allied night-fighters while flying over the Belgian town of Bastogne. There were no survivors. The lives of those men had been needlessly sacrificed – but at the same time the information they had brought to the Channel Islands from Granville had breathed new life and purpose into the massed ranks of fed-up German soldiers and their naval colleagues, who had been confined to port, no longer able to muster occasional forays against Allied shipping, since the islands' isolation from France. Luftwaffe units, too, anticipated a role, though it would not be in the air.

Liberated on 30–31 July 1944 by US soldiers of the 6th Armoured Division, the town of Granville had subsequently seen its small port assume strategic importance in the developing stages of the D-Day offensive. The dockside warehousing installed by the Americans, together with an impressive array of eighteen new cranes, underlined just how vital the harbour was to the Allies prior to the rehabilitation and reopening of larger ports captured, often at the expense of heavy damage to dockside infrastructure, in northern France. As the offensive gathered momentum and the availability of port facilities multiplied, Granville's importance had become increasingly focussed on the reception of coal shipments from England.

Organisation of the Granville raid is officially attributed to the 45-year-old recently promoted *Vizeadmiral* Friedrich Hüffmeier, a controversial figure who assumed overall armed forces command of the Channel Islands on 27 February 1945.[2] Prior to his islands posting in July 1944, his most prominent naval command had been with the battlecruiser *Scharnhorst*, between March 1942 and October 1943. Biographical accounts make clear that he was an unpopular master who commanded very little respect from the ship's company for the quality of either his seamanship or leadership.

While Hüffmeier may be credited with planning the raid on Granville, preparations for the assault had begun before his elevation to the supreme Channel Islands post, while he was acting as second-in-command to *Generalleutnant* Rudolf Graf von Schmettow, whose authority Hüffmeier, a fanatical Nazi, had repeatedly undermined in radio communication with his superiors in Berlin and elsewhere in the Reich. Typically, he sent a private letter in January 1945 to Admiral Theodor Krancke, commanding Naval Group West, outlining his proposals for an attack on Granville. Krancke evidently considered this a worthwhile gamble. He gave Hüffmeier the go-ahead and, with no shortage of volunteers among the critically under-employed forces on the islands, several hundred men were soon selected for special training in preparation for the raid.

However, in its first conception, the plan foundered. On the night of 6–7 February a raiding force composed primarily of patrol boats ran into thick fog soon after leaving St Helier. The mission was aborted and the flotilla told to return to harbour, though it seems it was a close-run thing for three patrol boats and a tug. Their skippers had not received the order to return and the four craft were desperately close to Granville before realising that the remainder of the flotilla had turned tail and gone back to Jersey. Some accounts describe how one of those raiding E-boats was intercepted by a US patrol craft on picket duty in the sheltered waters outside the harbour, protecting seven merchant vessels anchored to the southwest off Cancale, a port in the Ille-et-Vilaine department of Brittany. Indeed, awareness of the American ship's presence is another reason given by some sources for the late abandonment of the mission.

Clearly, warning of the predatory threat posed by the patrol ship, USS PC-552, had not reached the E-boat in time for her crew to take evasive action. The American ship opened fire and chased her all the way to a point west of Les Minquiers, from where the German vessel ramped up speed, unmatched by her pursuer, and without further obstruction made it home safely to St Helier.[3]

Hüffmeier was not put off. Now in overall control of the islands' military forces, he stepped up the training regime, basing his would-be commandos in Guernsey, the island furthest from prying Allied eyes, and was able to muster a more powerful flotilla for a renewed raid on the targeted port. Early in March he received Intelligence that a number of Allied ships were bound for Granville. Hüffmeier seized his chance. His upgraded assault force was readied for action.

Led by a seagoing tug, minesweepers (a quartet of the large M-class and two smaller R-class) were supported by three barges serving as gun boats, armed with 80mm cannons, a trio of the fast torpedo-equipped E-boats, two landing craft and a miscellany of fishing boats and harbour craft. Some reports suggest that the minesweepers' masts were removed to decrease the chances of radar detection. These details are taken from official American military sources, though estimates of the total number of craft involved, and the precise composition of the fleet, vary. Probably the landing craft (LCVP) stolen from the Americans and taken to Jersey by the five prisoners of war who escaped from Granville in December 1944 was utilised by the raiders and may have served as one of the three 'armed barrages.' It has been estimated by US chroniclers that some 600 men, possibly more, sailed with the raiding force. Placed in charge of this impressive assault group was *Kapitanleutnant* Carl-Friedrich Mohr, who had seen extensive wartime service with the German minesweeper fleet and was highly decorated – a holder of the Iron Cross 1st Class since August1940. Mohr was the ideal choice.

Unlike the attempt in February, which had at its sole objective the theft of whatever could be grabbed, the plan this time was multi-faceted. The taking of essential supplies remained at the heart of the operation but destruction now featured large, with ships berthed in the harbour – those that could not be plundered – targeted along with dockside installations and a radar post. Another objective for the assault force was to liberate compatriots from the prisoner of war camp and, if possible, take back some prisoners of their own, plucked from the battalion of American soldiers stationed in the area. It was ambitious in the extreme but it seems the flotilla sailed with the benefit of inside information from a local Frenchwoman, apparently an established collaborator, who worked at Granville's beachfront Hotel des Baines, serving in 1945 as a 'rest hotel' for American officers. Her knowledge of the guest list there and more generalised Intelligence on the deployment of the US forces at Granville promised a great deal.

It was dark, just, on the evening of 8 March when the raiding force slipped out of St Helier. The accounts of what happened next vary in their detail but the substance is generally agreed. American sources describe how, around midnight, two of the larger minesweepers split from the flotilla to take up defensive positions between Jersey and the Cotentin (Cherbourg) peninsula, ready to intercept any enemy craft coming down from the north. Shortly afterwards, the three armed barges assumed their allotted positions in the open waters outside Granville Harbour, lying in wait between the isles of Chausey, eleven miles to Granville's west, and the port town of Saint-Malo on the Brittany mainland, eighteen miles south of the small archipelago. From there the artillery barges were well placed to shell the Granville docks.

The enemy, however, was lurking. A coastal steamer at anchor on the other side of Chausey was protected by an armed trawler. Nearby, the US submarine-chaser PC-564 was patrolling the area. Unaware of the threat, the remainder of the German force closed in on Granville. As the tug and the two other large minesweepers headed for the harbour entrance, the three

E-boats made for the beach at the Hotel des Bains while another group prepared to attack the radar installation further up the coast. Brendan McNally, a US journalist and author who specialises in defence matters, has described in a comprehensive account of the Granville assault how luck was firmly on the side of the raiders when the tug and minesweepers were spotted by the American harbour authorities, who naturally challenged their right to enter the harbour by flashing a coded identification signal. 'Not knowing the proper response, the lead vessel's signalman simply flashed back the same signal,' wrote McNally in a 2013 online feature, *The Granville Raid*.[4] 'To their surprise, the harbourmaster accepted it and they entered without further challenge.

There were five merchant ships at the tiny harbour's brightly illuminated dockside. It was apparent that coal was being unloaded from one of these. The three German vessels sailed past, reaching sufficient clear space to come alongside. 'Immediately, seventy commandos jumped off and within a few minutes had secured the whole area,' McNally's dramatic account continued. The coal ships were the immediate priority. Boarding parties swarmed all over them. It triggered an immediate response – the crews were not about to surrender their vessels without a fight. So the shooting began with an exchange of small arms fire. Aboard the *Kyle Castle*, one of a quartet of small British freighters which made up the bulk of the docked Allied ships, the second officer tried desperately to mount a machine gun. He became the first casualty, shot and seriously wounded before he could activate the weapon. An officer's resistance aboard another of the British ships, the *Neptune*, ended similarly. The Germans soon had the freighters in their hands. The crews were told to ready their ships for an immediate get-away. When the *Kyle Castle's* skipper protested, he was shot. He died instantly, the first fatality. McNally drily observed that 'there were no more objections after that.'

Simultaneously, the men aboard the E-boats dispatched to the beach fronting the Hotel des Bains had met with little resistance, effectively capturing the hotel soon after coming ashore in inflatable craft. American losses were restricted, with two marines killed defending the hotel, but three officers were quickly taken prisoner and marched down to the shore. Some US sources suggest that, thanks to information gleaned from staff at the hotel, the nine most senior American military personnel in the town were rounded up and taken away by the raiders. They would have been well aware of the growing intensity of gunfire as US and French troops engaged the raiders – in the harbour itself and around the hotel – in a fierce exchange. There was action, too, outside the harbour entrance as sub-chaser PC-564 opened fire on the German artillery barges with a volley of star shells designed to illuminate their position.

Luck again favoured the raiders. The shells failed to explode in the air. Then, critically, the American vessel's deck-mounted gun jammed. All but defenceless, PC-564 succumbed to a fierce onslaught from the barges which destroyed the wheelhouse, damaged the ship elsewhere and killed around fourteen of her crew. The sub-hunter was forced into a desperate retreat back to the French coast where, pursued by the Germans, her skipper, Lieutenant Percy Sandell, grounded her on the Brittany shore at Pierre de Herpin light. Fifteen members of the US crew had prematurely abandoned ship. All but one were captured. Those who remained on board the stricken vessel, including Sandell, were later taken off safely by Allied colleagues.[5]

Ashore, despite increasingly heavy enemy fire, the Germans not only succeeded in freeing a large number of prisoners from the internment camp – estimates vary from fifty-five to seventy-nine – but rounded up as many as thirty Allied prisoners, mostly Americans, to take with them, a figure believed to include the fourteen crew members captured from sub-hunter PC-564. On the dockside, demolition charges and booby trap devices were laid. Everything was going to plan. Then, as the Germans aboard the coal ships attempted to coordinate their departure, the plan fell apart owing to a miscalculation, exacerbated no doubt by the Allied resistance and the time it had taken to deal with the threat of PC-564. The tide had turned – literally. The keels of all but one of the five merchant ships were stuck firmly on the seabed.

Propellers churned, but to no avail. Those ships were going nowhere; there simply was not enough water. The only exception was the partly-unloaded British collier *Eskwood*. It would be possible to take her under tow back to Jersey along with her six-man crew, a further contribution to the overall number of Allied personnel taken captive. Deprived of their booty from the other vessels – the British merchantmen *Kyle Castle, Neptune* and *Parkwood* and the Norwegian ship *Helen* – the frustrated German raiders did the next best thing. They all but blew them up, effectively sinking the British trio and seriously damaging the *Helen*.

The low tide also proved an impenetrable barrier to the raiding party sent to attack the radar facility. They were unable to get close enough to land their assault parties. Worse, minesweeper M-412 *De Schelde*, which went with them, ran aground in the shallows. It had to be abandoned and then blown up by its crew. Soon afterwards, the order to withdraw from Granville was given. Carl-Friedrich Mohr's swashbuckling assault force headed back to Jersey.

In their wake the raiders left a scene of devastation. Apart from the Allied ships, several of the dockside cranes, locks, a railway locomotive, rail wagons and ancillary equipment had either been destroyed or damaged. Twenty-two Allied personnel had been killed in the fighting – mostly Americans, but also including a Royal Navy officer and five British seamen – compared with just six fatalities on the German side. All but a dozen of the German servicemen freed from the PoW camp had been safely embarked, together with the captured Allied personnel, some reportedly paddled out to the waiting tug by a section of the raiding force. The capture of the *Eskwood* and the 112 tons of coal plundered from her hold was a decent return for the operation's principal objective, one that was more than matched by the psychological boost it undoubtedly delivered to the stranded occupying force in the islands.

Four days later Mohr's outstanding leadership was recognised when he was awarded the Knight's Cross of the Iron Cross, the highest military honour – with the single exception of the Grand Cross awarded to Herman Göring, Hitler's deputy – available under the Third Reich.

Of course, the operation was of little real significance. The war was lost. Two months later it would be formally concluded. Yet the Granville raid, though relatively small in scale, stands as one of Nazi Germany's final military triumphs. It cannot be disputed that it *was* a success and, while it could be argued that it did not conform to the strictest definition of a commando offensive – those who took part were regular service personnel, not elite forces specially trained over an extended period for such missions

– there is no doubt that the raiding party did receive some training to equip them for a commando-style operation against the French port.[6]

The evidence, while not conclusive, points to this being the 'splendid raid' mentioned by Robert Laycock in his 1947 RUSI lecture rather than any assault on an Isle of Wight radar station.

Certainly, we can conclusively remove from the equation the possibility that another assault by German occupation forces in the Channel Islands, several times mentioned in post-war narratives, was launched against the Isle of Wight – despite the fact that the Nazi authorities were very keen to convey widely the impression that offshore Wight was indeed the target. This was a mock assault, one that was actually mounted against the tiny Channel Island of Herm.

Lying three miles from the east coast of Guernsey, and, since 1949 when it was purchased from the Crown, forming part of Guernsey's bailiwick, Herm is just 1.5 miles long (north-south) and less than half-a-mile wide (east-west). When the Germans claimed this remote outpost in July 1940 its population numbered precisely two – the island's resident caretaker, Francis (Frank) Dickson, who so fascinated the newcomers they nicknamed him Robinson Crusoe, and his wife! The occupying force had little use for Herm. They built a small flak battery on the island and laid mines but, other than trips from Guernsey to shoot rabbits and boost the dwindling food supply, the German garrison largely ignored the place. There was, however, one major exception to this rule. It took place in late August/early September 1940, when an infantry force crossed from Guernsey to stage a mock seaborne landing, using motor boats and rubber dinghies, on the expansive sandy west coast beach at Shell Bay. A film unit accompanied the soldiers. When the resultant footage was edited it was given a title that was both sensationally stirring and deliberately wholly misleading – *The Invasion of the Isle of Wight*.

While the mock assault on Herm may also have served as part of rehearsals for the planned invasion of the UK, the film was, of course, an exercise in Nazi propaganda, intended for cinema audiences back in Germany and across occupied Europe – apparent proof that the invasion of Britain was under way. Whether the Germans planned to release the film as soon as the invasion was a reality or to 'jump the gun' and show it anyway, confident that the invasion would very soon be a reality, is unclear. There are certainly indications that it was screened, and even a suggestion that it was shown at Guernsey's Gaumont cinema in St Peter Port (since replaced by a bank) before December 1940 – though it is tempting to conclude that anyone with local knowledge would not have been fooled into confusing the sand dunes of Herm with the Isle of Wight's most probable landing beach for an invasion fleet at Sandown Bay.

As a post-script, confusion there most certainly was in December 1940 when a small party of foreign nationals thought they *had* landed on the Isle of Wight. On the 13th of that month, an unlucky Friday as it turned out, sixteen young Frenchmen, intent on fleeing occupied Brittany to join the Free French forces in England, set out in an open boat from the port of Dourduff hopeful of reaching the English south coast undetected by the Germans. Their intrepid secret mission was thwarted by bad weather, which knocked out their navigational equipment in the rough sea, and by a false sense of optimism when they waded ashore on reaching landfall with a lusty rendition of *La Marseillaise*, convinced they were in the Isle of Wight. Sadly for them, it was actually Vazon Bay in Guernsey. They were quickly captured by occupation forces.

Some have suggested this poignant tale may have given rise to the story of a German landing on Wight. This would surely require a very great deal of post-war confusion – the wrong island; the wrong nationality. It is of course a quite separate story and, tragically, one with the saddest of endings. Transferred by the Germans to Jersey, the young Frenchmen were tried by a military court early in 1941. Most were sent to prison, ending up in a German PoW camp. However, having been identified as their ringleader, François Scornet, aged just twenty, was sentenced to death. On 17 March he was shot by a firing squad in the grounds of the island's St Ouen's Manor. A memorial marks the spot where Scornet, a national hero in France, died.

Chapter 3

Radar on the Wight: Developing the Vital Shield

L ocal folklore on the Isle of Wight varies in its stories of a German commando raid. All versions agree that the attack was launched against one of the radar stations on the island's southern coast – but which one? Sometimes put forward as a possible location is RAF Ventnor's Chain Home (CH) station on the summit of St Boniface Down, the first on the island, the most prominent and, largely because there is still a radar facility there today (though now under civil control), easily the best-known. The favoured alternative lies three miles to the west, the former RAF St Lawrence, initially conceived as a mobile reserve facility for Ventnor. Before any consideration of hard evidence, the latter stands as the far more likely option for a seaborne landing – nobody is suggesting they came by air – by the enemy.

The comparative geographical characteristics of the two locations are obvious pointers. Constructed in the Isle of Wight's south-eastern corner, within a few feet of St Boniface Down's absolute summit – at 791 feet this is the highest point on the island – and the best part of a mile inland from the nearest stretch of coastline, RAF Ventnor would have presented a highly daunting challenge to a raiding force whichever way they approached it from the sea. If, as sometimes suggested, Wheelers Bay was the raiders' landing site, due south of the radar station, immediately northeast of Ventnor's seafront (see map), this would have necessitated an initial climb from the shore and, even under the cover of darkness, a potentially high-risk flirtation with the town's residential streets before the taxing ascent of St Boniface Down itself in order to reach the high-level radar compound, protected by a variety of defensive features.

In contrast, the radar station at St Lawrence, overlooking Woody Bay, stood just forty-four feet above the sea lapping at the foot of not especially steep cliffs. The approach to the pebbly beach would have meant rocky, but not insurmountable, obstacles to a cautious, well-prepared German force, even one arriving, as they certainly would have done, by night. To reduce the likelihood of detection from the guarded radar post and Ventnor, feasible alternative landing sites existed slightly further to the west at both Binnel Bay and Puckaster Cove. Looked at from the geographical perspective alone, ignoring strategic considerations, the odds would seem to fall heavily on the side of RAF St Lawrence as the more probable target.

The optional case for RAF Ventnor as the objective has been clouded in recent years by online forum discussion drawing attention to the 'fact' that the lofty site was chosen for a mock attack by a British commando force prior to the successful February 1942 raid on the German radar station at Bruneval in northern France. The possibility here (examined in chapter 4) is that this apparent 'dry run' may have contributed to the rumours of a real German raid.

That said, there can be little doubt that Ventnor, despite, or perhaps because of, the difficulties of access, would have been regarded by the enemy as a demonstrably greater 'scalp' for a landing party intent on making a bold statement of capability and symbolic menace. It will thus be important, later, to consider the overriding motives for a German attack.

In order to place the legendary Isle of Wight raid in its full context, it is helpful to review the early history of wartime radar on the island as a whole – in essence, a microcosm of the nation's overall development of radio detection fnding (RDF) following the experimentation and trials at Orford Ness and Bawdsey Manor outlined in chapter 1. The island story starts with the establishment of RAF Ventnor as the most westerly of the original twenty Chain Home stations planned by the Air Ministry in 1937 for use around England's eastern and southern coasts.

Although it was not the first site selected for the purpose – the nearby hills above St Catherine's Point, the island's southern-most tip, were originally earmarked by the Ministry – the top of St Boniface Down, on land requisitioned by the government from the National Trust in 1938, was a well-chosen location in all but one respect. Its summit offered the prospect of excellent long-range performance but the lack of level ground in front of the projected aerials meant the station could not fulfil a height-finding role, the ability to measure accurately the altitude of approaching enemy aircraft. This drawback would need later remedy.

Based, as were the others in the initial chain, on the design of the experimental station at Bawdsey, the plans for RAF Ventnor aimed to equip the site with transmitter aerials suspended from four 365-foot steel masts erected 180 feet apart, together with receiver aerials mounted on a quartet of 240-foot timber towers. The wooden construction of these towers was essential in order to avoid inhibiting the received signals – which would have been the likely outcome had steel towers been used instead. Plans for Ventnor's lofty site also provided for protected buildings to house the station's operating equipment in some degree of safety.

The worsening crisis in continental Europe which followed the ill-fated Munich Agreement at the end of September 1938 saw RAF Ventnor earmarked, along with seven other CH sites, for a quicker than planned operational introduction as an 'advance' station relying on experimental mobile transmitters, receivers and aerial equipment, with makeshift huts and power supplies. However, by the second week of November, with work progressing well on the 'final' station's wooden receiver towers, the plans for advance operation were bypassed as fitting-out began for Ventnor to move directly towards the status of an 'intermediate' station, with both transmitter and receiver aerials mounted on two of the wooden towers. The radar post was scheduled for commissioning during the final two weeks of January 1939. By the 17th of that month the aerials, supplied from Bawdsey, were in position and linked to the operating huts. Mains electricity had been laid on and the huts had been internally wired and powered.[1]

A commissioning team from Bawdsey were at the intermediate station between 15 and 18 January. Two days later, guarded by RAF personnel, the site welcomed its technical crew. Commissioning was completed by 26 January and the station was operational by the month's end. Two external telephone landlines – one underground – linked the station directly with London via, respectively, Ryde-Portsmouth and Newport/Cowes-Southampton. RAF Ventnor took part in trials to further the effectiveness of radar. These included the use in calibration tests of the earliest RAF Avro Rota version of the Cierva autogiro, named after its recently (in 1936) deceased Spanish designer, the renowned civil and aeronautical engineer Juan des la Cierva.

On Good Friday, 7 April 1939 the entire Chain Home network was placed on permanent 24-hour watch. In the months that followed, the four 365-foot steel transmitter towers required for RAF Ventnor's conversion to final operational status were erected, creating a riot of public speculation in the area as to their purpose, such was the secrecy which underpinned radar's introduction. Locally, the whole site was simply referred to as 'the pylons,' a catch-all name which was destined to stick.

It was, however, never going to be possible to hide the existence of such a distinctively prominent high-level installation from prospective enemy snoopers. That Nazi Germany knew of the station's development prior to Britain's declaration of war can be regarded as a certainty. St Boniface Down's emerging military 'secret' was clearly exposed from the air and duly photographed by those engaged in the Luftwaffe's thorough pre-war aerial reconnaissance survey of the British Isles, updated periodically once hostilities had commenced. There is also compelling evidence that the Nazis had their spies on the ground too.

There was, of course, nothing to stop German nationals, ostensibly visiting the UK in the late 1930s for holidays or sporting fixtures, from amassing information – in the shape of maps, photographs and picture postcards, or by the simple process of memorising topographical features – that might one day be of use to the Fatherland. There was official encouragement to do so. Certainly, teenagers from the Hitler Youth were on the Isle of Wight (as they were in other parts of the country) in 1937 for a cycling holiday, part of an apparently innocent initiative to foster links with Britain's Boy Scouts movement but one many in the UK were certain was designed to gather potentially valuable data for the regime in Berlin. The island base for the 'spyclists' – as the *Daily Herald* neatly branded them – was the YMCA at The Hermitage on St Catherine's Down, overlooking the Channel, close to the originally selected site for Ventnor's CH radar station. Whether Berlin was aware in 1937 of the likely establishment of radar in the area, or instinctively felt it a likely prospect, remains a moot point.

Anecdotal evidence clearly points to pre-war German interest in radar's developing presence. Sam Twining, whose grandmother owned much of the land on which RAF St Lawrence would later be built, recounts a particularly good tale which adds weight to the likelihood of prospective enemy Intelligence gathering as the initial station atop St Boniface Down took shape:

'I was on the beach at St Lawrence just after the war when my father was talking to Mr Blake, who had been given petrol for his boat during the war to pick up airmen – from both sides – who had come down in the sea off the local coast. One day he had picked up a German. Much to Mr Blake's surprise he had immediately recognised him. "I know you!" he said.

'The German, who spoke perfect English, replied that he was not surprised – he had stayed at Mr Blake's guesthouse before the war. "We were there to spy on your radar station," he told him!

'This was an obvious reference to the station on St Boniface Down [the only radar installation under construction on the island at the time]. "I've a good mind to throw you back in!" said Mr Blake before bringing the man ashore, where he was taken prisoner of war.'

In the second week of August 1939, RAF Ventnor, designated station 10 in the home chain numbering system, took part in the most extensive air defence exercises ever held in the UK. On the 24th, the issuing of the code-word *Afidock* put this vital link in the front line radar network onto a war footing. Ten days later, along with France, Britain declared war on Germany.

The home chain operated on wavelengths between five and fifteen metres. Ventnor's was set at 11.80. Its 'line of shoot' – the direction the station radiated its signal – was centred on 148 degrees over the English Channel to the south. In common with the other early CH stations, all of which faced out to sea with no rotating facility, Ventnor's was not equipped to continue the plot of enemy aircraft once they had passed overhead; from that point the task would be entrusted solely to the human resources of the Royal Observer Corps. A further limitation shared with others in the home chain was the inability to detect aircraft flying below 5,000 feet.

Despite these shortcomings, the station proved an effective cog in Britain's increasingly desperate defensive armoury once the all-conquering German military machine concentrated its focus in the summer of 1940 on knocking out British resistance, prior to planned invasion, in the wake of the extraordinary evacuation of Allied forces from the Dunkirk beaches and the catastrophic fall of France which followed on 14 June. The enemy was at the door. The Luftwaffe's job was to break it down. The RAF was in the front line. Early detection of Hermann Göring's aerial forces as they swept across the English Channel was vital.

It would be aided by a profound weakness in the enemy's knowledge of detailed British defensive strategy. In contrast to the pre-war precautionary reconnaissance and espionage, Germany, specifically its air force, suffered from a distinct lack of 'spies on the ground' once hostilities were under way. While the Nazis' military intelligence service, the Abwehr, did attempt to embed a string of agents in the UK during 1940, their attempts at infiltration were largely thwarted by a combination of internal rivalries, poor – to say the least – planning and thorough counter-intelligence. Thus, a broad knowledge of Britain's radar shield did not include an appreciation of how this was organised under the highly effective 'Dowding System,' the world's first large-scale use of a centralised command and control method of air defence. Named after Air Chief Marshal Hugh Dowding, head of RAF Fighter Command, the system combined reports from the radar stations and the Royal Observer Corps to orchestrate a unified means of directing interceptor aircraft and anti-aircraft artillery against incoming German plane

From the start of the Battle of Britain offensive on 11 July, the towering pylons on St Boniface Down played their part in alerting Fighter Command to the presence of large formations of enemy aircraft heading for southern England. The advanced British deployment of radar was proving its worth. Despite the Intelligence weakness, the Luftwaffe, used to operating in support of ground forces but now finding itself in an unaccustomed strategic role, was certainly aware of that. A month into the aerial battle, RAF Ventnor fell prey to its fury.

On 12 August the Luftwaffe, launching raids in large numbers against a range of targets in the southeast, delivered its first major blow against Britain's forward aerial defences. On a day which also saw attacks on three of Fighter Command's airfields in Kent, at Manston, Lympne and Hawkinge, the Germans targeted four of the RAF's Chain Home radar stations. Those in the south-eastern counties – at Rye and Pevensey, East Sussex, and

Dunkirk, Kent – suffered varying degrees of bomb damage, though none would be off the air for any appreciable time, but when the raiders attacked RAF Ventnor the outcome was far more serious.[2]

The radar station itself had earlier plotted the advance, as it passed over the Cherbourg peninsula, of a huge enemy force of more than 200 aircraft. Escorted by Messerschmitt fighter planes – twenty-five Bf-109s and 120 of the larger, twin-engine Bf-110s – were scores of Junkers Ju-88 bombers. As this fearsome formation approached Spithead in the eastern Solent and prepared to raid Portsmouth's strategic naval dockyard, its harbour and the city centre, a detachment of the Ju-88s turned tail and flew back across the Isle of Wight, headed for its south-eastern corner. For the first time in the war the island had been targeted for attack. Within minutes, the bombs were raining down on Ventnor's radar site from the first Ju-88s on the scene. Later arrivals, intercepted by Spitfires from the RAF's 152 and 609 squadrons, scrambled from their Dorset base at Warmwell – the former taking care of the bombers while the latter engaged their fighter escort – were denied the opportunity to add further damage. The devastation late on that fine Monday morning was bad enough without that.

What most sources say was fifteen planes, although others maintain it was as many as eighteen, swooped down from a height of around 10,000 feet, each of them dropping four high-explosive bombs on the radar station, which was also heavily machine-gunned by the aircraft. Despite a lack of available water on the hilltop, local fire crews battled valiantly to save what they could from the resultant conflagration but virtually all of the service buildings were effectively destroyed or rendered unusable. The human cost was mercifully light. No one was killed and the only reported injury at the radar site was to a soldier on station defence duties.

Inevitably, an air raid of this size was bound to cause a degree of what today would be classed as collateral damage. Several buildings in the Ventnor area suffered incidental damage. While in most cases this was not especially serious, two houses in the town's eastern district were badly affected by stray bombs and the damage to ceilings and windows at nearby Holy Trinity Church was deemed worthy of prominent coverage the following morning in the national press. Well documented, undisputed, without a shred of mystery, this was one German raid on the Ventnor area during the Second Wold War that is simple to assess.

Elsewhere on the island, aircraft from both sides crash-landed during the aerial battle which resulted from the raid. In the east of the isle, an RAF Spitfire was reported shot down on Bembridge airfield and a German aircraft at Ashey, near Ryde. The Luftwaffe had also lost a bomber near Godshill, northwest of Ventnor. Air Raid Precautions (ARP) headquarters in Newport reported that the Ju-88's pilot, *Oberst* Dr Johan-Volkmar Fisser, Commodore of the Orly-based KG51 bomber wing (the highest ranking Luftwaffe officer shot down on the island during the war), had burned to death despite a desperate attempt on the ground to save his life. His three colleagues had been captured and were in military custody. Meanwhile, on the mainland, the Germans' raid targets had also included the naval base at Portland, Dorset. Industrial concerns in both Portsmouth and Southampton (the Supermarine Spitfire works at Woolston among them) were additionally attacked by detachments of the large Luftwaffe force.

At RAF Ventnor, the need to clear several unexploded bombs at or near the radar site delayed the start of repair work but a total knock-out at was averted. The station was quickly back on air thanks to the use of mobile transmitting equipment in place of the site's transmitter block, a virtual write-off, and the early form of receiver apparatus which had been fitted as part of the station's intermediate phase. Operational reactivation, however, was short-lived, lasting only a matter of days. On Friday, 16 August, another frenzied day of activity in the sky above southern England, the enemy struck a second major blow. There would be no quick fix this time.

The previous day had seen the German air force attack in massed formations on a wide front, stretching right across the coastal belt of southern England and beyond. Considering the resources deployed, the relatively low rate of damage caused and the heavy losses it sustained, 15 August had proved a bitter disappointment for the Luftwaffe – its 'Black Thursday'. Göring's force had fallen victim to a combination of RAF resilience and its own strategic blundering. Revenge was in the air on the 16th and RAF Ventnor would feel the wrath.

Weather conditions were favourable that day for another massed German aerial attack. The tired pilots of RAF Fighter Command expected it and, at around midday, the CH radar stations on England's south coast detected enemy aircraft approaching across the Channel on three fronts. The most easterly formation was plotted off Dover, headed, it would soon transpire, for the Thames estuary. Three Fighter Command squadrons were scrambled to intercept a second, larger, force detected on an approach between Folkestone and Brighton. The fighting which followed was intense. Further west, the third formation, which had set out from Cherbourg, was on course for the Solent. East of the Isle of Wight the enemy force split up.

A large detachment of Junkers Ju-87s, the Stuka dive bombers first used to devastating effect in the Spanish Civil War, made for three targets. Despite heavy losses, a group of these greatly feared aircraft carried on a short distance to wreak havoc on the RAF's sector airfield at Tangmere while twenty dived on the Royal Naval Air Station at Lee-on-Solent (HMS *Daedalus*), just west of Gosport on the Solent's northern shore, damaging four hangars and forty-two aircraft. In the process, fourteen people were killed and five wounded. Meanwhile, the remaining Stukas had veered off to the left to begin a dive on Ventnor's damaged radar site.

At least seven high-explosive bombs (some sources suggest the number may have been significantly higher) were dropped during the subsequent five-minute strike by six of the Stukas, the trademark wail from their *Jericho-Trompete* (Jericho Trumpet) sirens an ominous precursor of doom. Two proved particularly destructive. As a result, all but two of the station's buildings above ground were unusable after the attack and every one of those below ground. The pylons themselves suffered serious damage. Repair work would be hampered, as it had been after the initial attack, by the priority task of clearing a number of unexploded bombs nearby, a situation which, as before, also temporarily closed the rail station 500 feet below.

This was definitely a knock-out blow. Ventnor's vital link in the radar chain was lost to the RAF. Its rehabilitation was essential but the damage was such that it would be more than two months before the station could be returned to operational use. Noting on reconnaissance missions the piles of debris deliberately left unattended on the site to fool them, the Luftwaffe initially was duped into believing RAF Ventnor had been abandoned altogether, never to re-open. By 23 August, the Germans had been disabused of any such notion, now convinced that the station was back on the air.

And, in a sense, it was. The enemy detected that the gap in the chain had been filled. They were right. However, it had been plugged not by a miraculously quick restoration of Ventnor's radar site but through the installation on the downs above Bembridge, ten miles to the northeast, of a mobile CH reserve facility, brought hastily to the Isle of Wight from London on 20 August to fill the void. It did so, albeit with unavoidably reduced operational range, until, early in November, the Ventnor site was passed fit to resume in full its front line duties.

By then, a direct line of covert information on the station to the Luftwaffe had been removed by the trial and imprisonment of George Wace Wall, a civilian technician at RAF Ventnor convicted of improperly recording secret data which would have been of benefit to the enemy. Wall's trial at the Old Bailey was held in camera, with press and public barred from the evidence. *The Times* of 19 September reported that Wall had been sentenced to six years' penal servitude after being found guilty on two counts of contravening the Official Secrets Act.

It has been said that, had Göring fully appreciated the extreme damage caused by his air force in its double strike on RAF Ventnor, and not been put off by its apparently speedy operational return, conjured up at Bembridge, he might have continued his strategy of attacking the British radar deterrent, in which case the outcome of the Battle of Britain, and the fate of Britain itself, might have been wholly different. The fact that he did not was a key error.

As it was, the *Reichsmarshall* stuck to his belief that 'it is doubtful if there is any point in continuing the attacks on radar sites in view of the fact that not one of those attacked has been put out of operation'. In fact, Göring had issued this change of strategy on 15 August, the day *before* the strike on Ventnor, as part of an eleven-point directive to all Luftwaffe commanders setting out his overall reappraisal of air force tactics. He wanted no more time wasted, as he saw it, on the British radar stations. As a result, Ventnor would remain the only one dislocated for any length of time from the chain during the course of the crucial aerial battle.

The possibility of further enemy attacks on the radar chain, however, was still a live issue in Britain. Motivated principally by Ventnor's protracted absence from the radar shield, but also by damage caused through enemy action elsewhere, notably at RAF Poling in West Sussex, heavily bombed on 18 August, the Air Ministry elected to provide many of the CH stations with buried reserve equipment, building transmitter and receiver blocks underground, linked to 120-foot wooden towers. Plans were put in place to equip Ventnor with the buried facility, though oddly it would be constructed within the same compound as the vulnerable and already targeted CH site itself. In *Radar on the Isle of Wight*, his 1994 book for the Historical Radar Archive in Lincolnshire, Mike Dean suggests this was not fully operational until well into 1942.

Also located within the Ventnor site was a self-contained radar facility installed by the British Army. This provided a CHL (Chain Home Low) function, initially introduced by the army as a system for detecting ships and later developed by the RAF with an inbuilt ability to detect aircraft flying at altitudes below the operating capabilities of the original Chain Home sites. Given the station name of Boniface Down, the CHL unit's formal numerical designation was M86 – CD/CHL Type 2, indicating, first, that it had a coastal defence (CD) role and, second, that it formed part of the second type of Air Ministry Experimental Station, or AMES, after the Type 1 stations of the first-generation Chain Home units. It appears to have opened in 1941.[3]

In May of the same year the first of several major upgrades to the main CH station saw an increase in the transmitting power output. This was to have a significant visual effect on the layout of the site. In order to cope with the much higher voltages, a new 'curtain array' aerial system was installed, slung between the steel masts. As a result, one of the four masts was no longer needed. It was subsequently dismantled and removed from the Isle of Wight for use elsewhere on the expanding chain in Scotland. Precisely where is unclear, It may, as most sources suggest today, have been repositioned at Skaw on Unst in the Shetland Isles or, as others have recorded, relocated in the Orkneys, either at Netherbutton or Sanday (Whale Head).

September 1941 saw a further change to the Ventnor's station's appearance when it was used to test Britain's new, and ultimately highly successful, Gee radio navigational system which measured the time delay between two radio signals in order to produce a 'fix' with accuracy in the order of a few hundred metres at ranges of up to 350 miles. The transmitter and receiver systems were housed during the Isle of Wight trial in wooden huts located close to their associated steel and wooden masts, rising respectively to 365 and 240 feet.

Another notable development provided Ventnor with height-finding capability via a system known as the variable elevation beam (VEB), developed in 1941 by scientists at the Telecommunications Research Establishment (TRE) and the Royal Aircraft Establishment (RAE) – a concept that did not require the extensive calibration process which bedevilled earlier systems. This entailed fixing a mechanically tilted aerial array on the face of one of the 240-foot receiver towers. The VEB was in operational use at Ventnor by the start of July 1942.

Already in place by that time was the RAF's development of the Royal Navy's Type 271 radar equipment, the first supplied to Ventnor to use centimetric, or microwave-band, technology. This was a significant addition to the St Boniface Down compound, the first CH site to receive it. Formally known as Type 273 Mark V, it presented Ventnor with the ability to track aircraft flying at altitudes even lower than a CHL's limits – all the way down to fifty feet – and small surface craft at long range with a degree of reliability hitherto unachievable. RAF development of the apparatus had started only in December 1941. By February 1942, the first set was in experimental use at Ventno, where it was colloquially referred to as the Ventnor HPT (high power transmitter). It featured a ten-foot diameter parabolic dish aerial mounted on a gantry straddling one-third of the Nissen hut which housed an operations room equipped with a plan position indicator (PPI), a cathode ray tube which displayed the relative positions of enemy aircraft and intercepting RAF fighters at the same time. Following the trials, a second, standby, rig of the same design was deployed at RAF Ventnor at the end of 1942.

Type 273 Mark V rigs would eventually be re-designated AMES Type 53, reflecting the standardised referencing of successive RAF radar systems with the AMES (Air Ministry Experimental Station) prefix originally applied solely to the original Chain Home installation at Bawdsey Manor during its pre-war occupancy by Robert Watson-Watt's development team.

A particularly irksome thorn in the flesh of the RAF, and Britain's defence in general, was the enemy's ability to jam the nation's radar shield with frequency modulating signals. A way round this was clearly needed and by the end of 1942 it arrived via the installation at Ventnor and five other CH sites of mobile Type 11 radar rigs. Cunningly, this new equipment was configured to operate on the same frequency as the Germans' own Wurzburg radar system in the, surely inarguable, belief that the enemy would not seek to jam its own radar shield! For this reason, the rotating Type 11 set was to be used sparingly, only in the direst of jamming emergencies, so that the Germans were given little opportunity to detect its secret presence. Equipped with a PPI, it possessed its own height-finding capability and was intended for use in a ground control interception (GCI) role, a key development in the radar war which also featured prominently elsewhere on the Isle of Wight and is described later in this chapter

In March 1942, the compound had acquired an example of the RAF's own centimetric radar design. The Type 13 CMH (centimetric-height) radar, an improved version of an earlier prototype, featured an advanced height-finding function. Both in appearance and operation this was highly distinctive kit. Fitted with a 'cheese aerial,' so called because its shape resembled that of a half-sliced cheese, the Type 13 CMH achieved impressive height-finding accuracy by rocking the beam up and down, a motion which gave rise to its 'nodding horror' nickname! Its introduction effectively spelt the end at Ventnor for the earlier VEB apparatus.

With RAF radar development proceeding at a swift pace, the Type 14 search radar, closely related to the Type 13, followed in mobile form during the spring of 1943.[4] This too featured a 'cheese aerial' but, unlike its vertical predecessor, it rotated in the horizontal position, providing Ventnor with the dual capacity for detecting both low-flying aircraft during daylight hours and long-range surface detection at night.[5]

As stated, RAF St Lawrence was originally conceived as the site for a mobile reserve facility for Ventnor, using equipment, including a 105-foot portable wooden mast, mounted on trucks and trailers. A more pressing need was identified by the Air Ministry in June 1941. On the mainland, to the west of the Isle of Wight in what is now part of Dorset, RAF Southbourne, near Bournemouth, had recently been added to the CH network. The station had been allocated provision for a remote reserve but efforts to find a suitable location within reasonable distance of the CH site had proved impossible.

Instead, it had been decided to locate it on the island at St Lawrence. 'The site is within a short distance of the CH station at Ventnor and, when needed, will be manned and maintained by Ventnor personnel,' noted the ministry.

Southbourne's reserve requirements may have been the principal motivation but it is clear that Ventnor's operational shortcomings and vulnerability were still key factors in the Air Ministry's plans for St Lawrence. Although the island's CH site had already been allocated its own buried reserve, the ministry had identified two reasons why St Lawrence would be useful in the Ventnor context. First, greatly helped by the presence of high hills to the north which served to block unwanted reflections (the return of electromagnetic waves), the new site would have the height-finding capability initially denied to Ventnor because of its uneven high-level terrain. Second, as the ministry now belatedly recognised, 'Ventnor was bombed out of action last year and it is feasible that this may happen again and that its buried reserve, which is not dispersed, may also suffer damage.'

Interestingly, Mike Dean's research for the Historical Radar Archive has revealed that, when first planned, the St Lawrence site had been referred to as 'Paradise,' probably after nearby Paradise Walk, a questionable, and apparently short-lived, name for a wartime deterrent despite its inarguably attractive coastal setting.[6] This was later matched in oddness by the station's official RAF designation. Southbourne remained the 'parent' site. As this was numbered 11 in the CH chain, St Lawrence would be known as station 11R instead of 10M, the number it had been destined to carry as Ventnor's mobile reserve.

It seems an obvious anomaly. The new station's position on the Isle of Wight now lay outside the geographical territory of the RAF signals wing (No. 76) which was both funding its construction via allocated resources and would control its operation. The situation was clarified on 25 February 1942 in a memorandum from Squadron Leader R.C. Cole at the headquarters of No. 60 (Signals) Group, which had overall responsibility for RAF radar. His memo made it clear that, 'for all purposes,' St Lawrence would be treated as an emergency alternative reserve (EAR) for RAF Ventnor and that responsibility for its operation would be transferred to signals wing 75, of which the latter already formed part.

RAF St Lawrence, therefore, would now serve as a full-time radar station in its own right. Its specific location on the low cliffs overlooking Woody Bay and the English Channel was on requisitioned arable land at and adjacent to Old Park Farm within the Undercliff, the long, dramatic tract of land in the island's far south nestling beneath the escarpment from which it takes its name. Those whose land was involved were not, of course, told the precise nature of the Air Ministry's plans for the site. Surviving correspondence reveals that they were advised the ministry was 'going to make some permanent erections of a highly secret nature' – for use both during and after the war.[7] By late July 1941, as this information was being relayed to landowners, work had already started on a concreted access to the site from the local road network.

Receiver and transmitter blocks, some 200 yards apart, were constructed, both covered in an earth mound for added protection. Alongside each was a 120-foot wooden aerial. Further inland, a standby set-house, similarly covered, was also provided to generate vital back-up electrical power for the site when required.[8] The station, however, was not equipped with any provision for accommodating its operatives. As planned from the outset, it was manned by personnel from RAF Ventnor, housed either at the St Boniface Down radar site or in two requisitioned hotels in St Lawrence village itself. The station's line of shoot was 170 degrees, twenty-two degrees more southerly than Ventnor's, a useful addition to radar coverage from the Isle of Wight. By1942 RAF St Lawrence was operating round the clock in permanent guise.[9]

Meanwhile, the island had acquired a further RAF radar station a few miles further west. The inception of RAF Blackgang, however, was for purposes wholly distinct from those which saw the establishment of the installations at Ventnor and St Lawrence. Blackgang was a ground control interception (GCI) station, part of an air defence system pioneered by the RAF as the war progressed. With the location of enemy aircraft identified by the Chain Home network forwarded via a sector control filtering process, the nearest GCI station was able effectively to control the course of an aerial battle from that early detection stage to the interception by RAF fighter planes of the incoming threat, leading Fighter Command's aircraft directly to the target. An integral aspect of the system was the use of the plan position indicator (PPI) described earlier. Another was the allocation to each station of specific 'resident' planes whose interceptions and routine patrols were guided throughout by the assigned GCI unit. Overall, this was a far-reaching breakthrough radar system in more ways than one.

GCI's introduction, which began in earnest from the spring of 1941, eliminated both the requirement for labour-intensive detection and plotting at different locations and the need for related communication links. Unlike the fixed installations at CH stations, the Type 8 radar in use at GCI sites could rotate through 360 degrees, an obvious aid in tracking incoming aircraft once they had passed over the coast. There were drawbacks with its initial use, however. The ability to turn the apparatus continuously was severely hampered by its mode of operation – a reliance on a bicycle-type drive mechanism which required the use of two men. Although mounted together on a single plinth, the aerial's transmitter and receiver components operated separately, with a consequent need to keep them exactly aligned on the same bearing – something of a challenge to GCI operatives when there was an appreciable wind.

RAF Blackgang, station 45G in the Air Ministry's numbering system, was located 470 feet above the sea on downland formerly used for farming. Half-a-mile inland from St Catherine's Point, the site overlooked the village of Niton. Jim Crofts was among the six airmen initially posted to the station in March 1941 and has written extensively about life at the unit. 'We were billeted with families in Niton so became very much part of the village scene,' he recalled. According to former RAF radar operative Don Adams, who has chronicled the story of the Ventnor area's radar sites for an online series, the station was 'certainly working effectively by 1942.' If this was the case, it appears to have shared a site, at least for a period, utilised by a mobile CHL (Chain Home Low) installation. Both Don Adams and Mike Dean, in his own study of Isle of Wight radar development, point to evidence which suggests the CHL apparatus was operational at Blackgang from March 1943.

'The station was manned for twenty-four hours a day and we worked on a three-watch system,' Jim Crofts remembered. This appears to have been a common arrangement at all GCI units, but each day would see one of the stations in turn switch off their radar equipment for a one-hour period of routine maintenance. This was almost certainly a key factor in a 'tip and run' attack by the Luftwaffe which came close to shutting down Blackgang altogether in 1943.

Such raids were characterised by a small number of aircraft flying in low to minimise the risk of radar detection before homing in on a target – often in a residential area – which was then attacked by each plane with cannon fire prior to the dropping of a single high-explosive bomb. The pilots wasted no time in getting away, tip and run raids often lasting no more than a minute from start to finish. They were a particularly nasty form of aerial warfare, stripped of any pretence of gallantry and designed principally to create terror among the civilian population. While none created as much mayhem and catastrophe among residents as an infamous air raid on major industrial concerns in the twin towns of Cowes and East Cowes in May 1942, during the mid-war period considerable damage and significant loss of life resulted from repeated tip and run raids on the Isle of Wight at Ryde, Newport, Shanklin and Ventnor.

Looking back in his November 2005 feature for the BBC's *WW2 People's War* website, Jim Crofts described how:

> 'for some months Blackgang had proved a thorn in the side of the enemy. Our record of successful interceptions was excellent and we had also been involved in anti-shipping operations at night with Albecore aircraft based at RAF Thorney Island [in which] enemy E-boats were intercepted as they returned from attacking our shipping in the Channel.'

However, unbeknown to RAF Blackgang and its sister stations, the Germans were monitoring transmissions from the other side of the Channel and had successfully worked out the sequence of the 'switch off' cycle. 'They knew exactly which unit was off the air,' added Jim Crofts.

The former fighter controller described how, at 10.30am on Tuesday, 1 June 1943, it was Blackgang's turn to switch off for maintenance. According to his story, this presented the enemy with 'an ideal opportunity to put RAF Blackgang out of business'. As the station's radar mechanics checked the vital parts of the system, non-technical staff tidied up the operations block while others attended to routine tasks elsewhere on the site. They were halfway through the maintenance period when, suddenly, they heard the roar of low-flying aircraft and what sounded like a series of explosions in nearby Niton village. It was soon obvious that the Luftwaffe had launched one of its familiar low-level tip and run attacks on the area.

Added Jim Crofts:

'A few more explosions were heard and in a very short time all was quiet. "Are they regrouping for another attack?" we thought. It must be their plan to destroy the radar station next! However, nothing materialised and we all emerged from our sheltering positions to see a pall of smoke rising from the area just south of the radar unit.'

The raiders had fled.

Taking advantage of low cloud cover, eight Fw-190 single-engine fighters had swooped in on Niton to mount the raid. Whether or not their target was the radar station remains an arguable point. It might instead have been the close-by coastal radio station or, possibly, this was yet another deliberate attack on a residential area, though Jim Crofts is not alone in insisting the Germans had decided 'the [radar] station must be eliminated' when they crossed the Channel that morning. It is hard today to determine the truth of this. As it turned out, it was the Undercliff Hotel which suffered the most. A bomb from one of the marauding aircraft scored a direct hit on the large building, completely destroying it. The hotel had been used as a wartime billet for military personnel and two soldiers were among the raid's fatalities, giving rise to another theory that this might have been the principal intended target all along – or one of them.

Rescue parties toiled all afternoon to extricate others from the wreckage of the hotel. There was nothing they could do, however, for the three keepers of the lighthouse at St Catherine's. When the Luftwaffe attacked, by a cruel twist of fate the men were together in the emergency power house and boiler room, carrying out an annual routine of stacking migratory bird perches which they had just taken down from the adjacent tower. Possibly mistaken for a radar installation – a further variation often suggested for the raid's objective – the outbuildings received a direct hit. All three keepers were killed. However, while the explosion also badly affected the nearby principal keeper's cottage, the lighthouse tower itself escaped with relatively minor blast damage. It seems this was not in the German pilot's target sights that fateful morning.

It is a sad truth that, had one or more of the keepers been at work inside the tower, as normally would have been the case, their lives would have been saved. As it was, the three men, principal keeper Richard Grenfell and his assistants, Charles Tompkins and William Jones, were buried in the nearby church at Niton. Poignantly, in the lighthouse tower superficial damage to the lantern, caused by flying glass shards from blast-shattered windows, is still evident today, presenting no detrimental effect to the now automated light's efficiency.

A sixth fatality was an elderly local man whose home near the village school also took a direct hit. A further eleven people were injured. Among these was Leading Aircraftwoman Sheila Barnard, an off-duty radar operative from RAF Blackgang. Jim Crofts described how she survived a bizarre experience when leaving the Buddle Inn at Niton Undercliff, unaware of the impending raid.

'A Fw-190 dropped its bomb in the driveway of the inn but, because it was delivered from such a low angle, the bomb incredibly skipped on the drive, knocked Sheila over and continued, *Dambuster* fashion, for another 200 yards before it exploded in a field … Sheila had been knocked against a stone wall … remarkably, although she had suffered a nasty break to her left arm, [she] was alive and was quickly conveyed to the [Royal National] hospital outside Ventnor.'

Several other buildings in the area were damaged but, while a window at Niton's parish church was smashed in the aerial attack, remarkably it turned out to be the only one not made of stained glass! Maybe, as some would later have it, this was a sign from above that enough was enough. It turned out to be the last tip and run raid against the island.

Indeed, never again would the radar sites in the south of the Isle of Wight be in the firing line of aerial attacks by the Luftwaffe. However, these were not the only radar installations on the island. For the sake of completeness, any examination of the local radar defences in the years and months leading up to the summer of 1943, the period of the war most often quoted for the long-rumoured German seaborne raid, should also take into account the development and deployment by the various armed forces of Britain's early warning shield elsewhere on the isle.

Among these was the CD/CHL station at The Needles, established by the army in June 1941 to provide direction control for the two batteries (Old Needles and New Needles) on the far-western headland. Without disrupting the station's coastal defence function, the site's manning and maintenance was taken over by the RAF at the end of that year under a 'triple service' agreement, following initial concern that the rig was incapable of aircraft detection, and a subsequent upgrading by the army. This meant that, through the use of two separate cathode-ray tube (CRT) consoles, both army and navy operatives were able to watch for surface threats while the RAF kept an eye on aircraft flying at lower altitudes, forwarding detected tracks to RAF Ventnor on St Boniface Down. In each case the effective range was around thirty miles. By the end of 1942, the Royal Navy had assumed control of all surface traffic, although by then this was on a standby basis only, the army having relinquished its role.

Determining wartime radar configurations can prove something of a challenge, often riddled with confusing sets of historical data. The equipment employed at The Needles is a case in point. While the rig in use there was known as Type 41 by the RAF, according to Don Adams it was actually the Royal Navy's Type 271 Mark V kit 'in a fixed cabin with a rotatable parabolic dish aerial,' sited sixteen feet above the cliff-top, which itself was 400 feet above the sea.[10]

At the opposite end of the Isle of Wight radar was a factor in the extensive wartime defences on and around the high downs overlooking Bembridge, the island's easternmost village. Reference has been made already to the installation here of mobile Chain Home apparatus as temporary replacement for RAF Ventnor's bombed-out station in the late summer of 1940. However, by that time development of the radar shield was already under way in the area. In May 1940, the government's Air Defence Research and Development Establishment at Christchurch was told to rig up Chain Home Low equipment for use by the Coast Artillery Experimental Establishment set up by the army at the nineteenth century Yaverland Battery, on the lower slopes of Bembridge Down, close to the seaside town of Sandown. The instruction was a key component of tests to establish the coastal defence capabilities of CHL radar.

By mid-June, a site for trial, and hopefully operational, use of the equipment had been chosen close to the 9.2-inch gun battery at Culver Down. The experimental station's two aerial arrays were mounted on wooden towers. With the base level just short of 290 feet above sea level, the towers rose a further sixteen feet to the level of the aerials. Apart from testing the general effectiveness of its coastal defence role, the trail-blazing CHL set was also used to investigate the side-effects of the nearby guns, as well as the ground configuration, on the radar's azimuth (compass bearing) accuracy. Errors were detected but, while the guns were found to have very little detrimental effect, it was concluded that variations in the slope of the ground were probably the main cause of the problem. The presence in the area of seaside piers at Sandown and Shanklin, which produced echoes in the side lobes of the radar picture, was another complicating factor, as was that of nearby Fort Bembridge, which appeared in the back lobes. Together, this amounted to a significant amount of unwanted 'clutter' on the screen.

Trials with detecting surface vessels from Culver also proved unsatisfactory owing to the seriously interfering presence on the radar picture of further 'clutter.' Although the equipment was employed, with some success, for night operational use early in July, the decision was taken soon afterwards to move the CD/CHL rig to the west and re-position it within the confines of Fort Bembridge, some 1,500 yards back from Culver's headland battery.

Another of the Isle of Wight's many defences built in the 1860s to safeguard Spithead, the Solent's eastern approaches and Portsmouth against perceived French aggression, Fort Bembridge was located on higher ground than the Culver site, near the summit of Bembridge Down. As a battery observation post, its principal military function during the Second World War was a co-ordinating role for the heavy coastal gun sites in the island's northeast, notably at nearby Culver and Nodes Point, St Helens. The fort also provided barracks accommodation for army gunners and housed a Royal Navy contingent engaged in the business of submarine detection.

The radar rig re-positioned at the fort stood 343 feet above the sea and was assigned the station number 10A in the Chain Home Low series, with its female WAAF radar operatives billeted close by, but far below, in Sandown.[11] The fort's ramparts were used to house both transmitter and receiver, but while the former was located within a light bomb-proof cell, use of one of the existing structural features was made for the receiver, more sturdily protected inside a former ammunition store. The tower-mounted aerial arrays protruded some way above the outer walls and were thus only marginally less visible than they had been on Culver Down.

In its new location, the rig was operational from 30 July 1940 and was again used for a range of trials as experimentation with the CD/CHL concept progressed, work which helped refine specifications and deployment. In August 1941, as part of a general upgrade for CHL radar, the Air Ministry announced that the Bembridge rig was to be transferred once more, although this time it would be a short move to new accommodation within the fort. The equipment was enhanced at this stage, the improvements including a common aerial instead of the previous two and the installation of PPI apparatus to bring the rig up to improved technical standards. This was followed, six months later, with a power-turning facility for the aerial array.

Mike Dean records how the upgraded Bembridge radar 'played a small part' in the operations of 11–13 February 1942 when the twin German battlecruisers *Scharnhorst* and *Gneisenau*, the heavy cruiser *Prinz Eugen* and the trio's escort ships escaped from the occupied French port of Brest, famously evading for an extended period a British blockade in the Channel. They were able to remain undetected for thirteen hours partly through the heavy jamming of tracking radar screens in the UK. However, mid-morning on 12 February the CHL station at Bembridge detected several hostile aircraft at a range of 129 miles and plotted their track for the next 190 miles. At a later board of enquiry ordered by an unhappy Churchill – there had been a high number of casualties and losses on the British side in the eventual engagement – it emerged that those Luftwaffe planes had been circling in a small area above the German ships![12]

Least known, and most inland, of all the Isle of Wight's radar installations was an army-operated rig set up during 1941 in the east of the island at Hale Common, between the villages of Arreton and Apse Heath. Originally a mobile facility, its receiver and transmitter were mounted on lorries, and the aerials were initially turned by hand before an electrical motor took over.

Then, in great secrecy during the winter of 1942–43, it was moved a short distance south, re-locating in more permanent form, with its equipment housed in concrete buildings and its operatives in nearby Nissen huts, on an isolated rural site at Macketts Farm.

Geoffrey Searle, who worked at the site as a radar mechanic with the Royal Electrical and Mechanical Engineers (REME), recalled:

'The idea of the radar was to provide an early warning for the gun operations rooms at both Newport and Fareham [Hampshire]. They would notify the various local gun sites and the guns could then be trained on the target before it reached the area. We were plotting up to a 45-mile radius from the site. The aerial turning gear was in a big underground compound, with just the aerials themselves showing above ground – thirty-two of them.'

The seven REME mechanics at the site, supervised by a solitary sergeant, were joined by twenty-six ATS women operators and a six-man artillery guard.

'We all had to sign the Official Secrets Act on taking up our post,' added Geoffrey Searle when interviewed in 1989. Fortunately for him, the secret radar installation was the perfect posting as he was himself an islander.

'My family knew nothing more than I was working on a radar site "somewhere", although I was able to go home, to Ryde, every night. The public never came anywhere near us. We were issued with a machine gun for our direct defence only. On one occasion, when a low-level German force attacked Ryde in 1943, it passed immediately overhead, but we weren't allowed to fire – that would have given the game away.'

Taking all this into account, it can be said that at the time of the legendary raid by sea in the summer of 1943 the Isle of Wight, tantalisingly close in relative terms, offered potentially 'rich pickings' for an enemy anxious to keep abreast of Britain's constantly developing radar shield. The possibility of a seaborne raid from an inquisitive foe was a constant threat – but is there any specific evidence to suggest such an attack on the island was expected in 1943? A document preserved at the National Archives hints that this might have been the case.

It is in the form of a memorandum, marked 'secret' at the time, compiled by the Telecommunications Research Establishment which in May 1942 had moved from its Dorset base at Worth Matravers, near Swanage, to a new home at Malvern College, Worcestershire. The memo records the results of a TRE watch at RAF Ventnor for 'unusual signals' during the period between 11 March and 3 April 1943. Although the target sweep did extend as far to the southeast as enemy-held coastal territory between Le Havre and Calais, it was mainly concentrated to the south and southwest, enveloping the Channel Islands and the Normandy-Brittany coast between the Cotentin peninsular and Lannion in the Côtes-d'Armor. The watch was aimed at tracking signals associated with a variety of equipment, including any German use of the air-to-surface vessels (ASV) airborne radar system for detecting ships at sea.

Signals from the Germans' many Freya and Wurzburg radar sites in France, by then well-known to the British (see chapter 4), were disregarded, the memo records, 'since they are adequately covered by "Y" stations' – Britain's network of signals intelligence collection sites.

Was this watch by the TRE boffins, no doubt using state-of-the-art tracking technology, the result of specific intelligence suggesting a German strike was imminent, or at least in prospect, in retaliation for the raid on Bruneval's radar a year earlier? Or was the Ventnor operation pursued with a more generalised aim of seeking out previously undetected forms of enemy signals traffic? It remains an arguable point. What is clear is that the 1943 watch revealed nothing of note. 'In spite of an intensive, although sometimes spasmodic, search, no unusual signals were heard which could not be traced to friendly sources,' the TRE memo adds.[13]

It is tempting to conjecture that, had the TRE's Ventnor watch been carried out a few months later, it might have stood a better chance of detecting signals revealing imminent enemy action.

Chapter 4

Operation Biting: Chewing Over the Wight Links

The suggestion is often made that the rumoured seaborne raid on an Isle of Wight radar station was a 'tit for tat' mission organised by Germany in response to the highly successful tripartite British assault on the Bruneval radar installation in occupied northern France. Formally known by the codename Operation Biting, the Bruneval raid took the enemy by surprise on the night of 27–28 February 1942. It delivered a desperately-needed boost for the British war effort at a particularly difficult period, and for the army's newly-developed force of paratroopers at the heart of the operation, a first, and rightly highly acclaimed, battle honour.

If Germany did mount a raid against offshore Wight in the summer of 1943 as a specific act of reprisal for Bruneval, it has to be said it took them a while to get around to it. Nonetheless, it is worth taking a look at Operating Biting in a search for parallels with, or possible motivation for, the rumoured attack on British soil. Caution is needed in any such exercise, however. It is possible that Bruneval has been 'paired' with the Isle of Wight story in the way it has because of another suggested link between the two in the run-up to the 1942 Biting assault.

It is a link which, if true, also opens up the possibility that it might have been, in part at least, the very basis for the emergence of the Isle of Wight's enduring 'raid on the radar' legend itself.

Scottish writer and war veteran George Millar's absorbing 1974 book, *The Bruneval Raid: Stealing Hitler's Radar,* first published by Book Club Associates via an arrangement with The Bodley Head in London, and held by many to be the most authoritative account of the famous mid-war assignment, was prefaced by a foreword from Louis Mountbatten, Chief of Combined Operations at the time it was carried out. He saw Millar's work as 'a further opportunity to pay a tribute to the brilliant planners and the gallant men who made such a success of the raid'. Yet neither Mountbatten's foreword nor the author's narrative mentioned an aspect of the story which others have since maintained was a key part of the planning for Biting.[1]

Internet references to the claimed link – and there are many of them – basically follow the same lines. Indeed, they are all but identical, suggesting that they arise from a single common source. As so often happens, this story has been repeated so many times it has acquired the cloak of authority and yet, plausible though it remains in outline, it is difficult to find any credible corroborative evidence with which to underpin it. The online references do not list the ultimate external source. Most refer the reader solely to a review of Isle of Wight radar during the Second World War, most recently updated in 2007, on the h2g2.com website as the originating channel for the story. A British-based collaborative encyclopaedia project providing, in its own words, 'an unconventional guide to the universe and everything', the website operates in the spirit of *The Hitchhiker's Guide to the Galaxy* from the science fiction comedy series of the same name by Douglas Adams, first broadcast as a radio programme in 1978 and later adapted for television and other media. So is the site's Bruneval story itself fiction?

The oft-quoted reference claims, correctly, that between 1940 and 1942 Britain was determined to find out exactly how far advanced was German radar. To this end a raid was planned on a recently discovered example of Germany's Würzburg arrays – a development in the enemy's radar shield confirmed in Britain thanks to some remarkable photo-reconnaissance – near the village or Saint-Jouin-Brunevel, around fifteen miles north of Le Havre.

With arguably less regard for descriptive accuracy, the website reference adds that, 'to ensure success, a mock raid was made at an almost identical, externally, radar station in Britain – that of Ventnor on the Isle of Wight.' In reality, neither in terms of outward appearance or specific geographical location could the radar sites at Bruneval and Ventnor be described as 'almost identical.' The claim that they were might seem to undermine the credibility of the mock raid story, though this is probably an unfair assessment. In terms of the two stations' strategic use, close to the coastal fringes of France and Britain respectively, similarities certainly did exist. Exaggeration is the probable culprit. The story cannot be summarily dismissed.

The tale is not lacking in detail. It continues:

'Without warning, No. 2 Special Service Battalion, under the command
of Colin Newman, undertook a night raid and successfully penetrated
the outer minefield and other defences, bursting into the operations
room and then putting stickers on equipment which, if it had been a
real raid, they would have taken for study.'

None of the authors of books on Operation Biting published since George
Millar's 1974 account are any more illuminating on the suggestion of a
practice raid at Ventnor. In the context of preparations for Bruneval, there is
no mention of Ventnor, let alone its radar station, or indeed the Isle of Wight
as a whole, and no reference to an army officer called Colin Newman, in any
of them. No. 2 Special Service Battalion was one of five battalions, formed
by volunteers form other army units, which in November 1940 had been
organised into Britain's Special Service Brigade for commando training.
Commandos did take part in Operation Biting. However, while they were
initially considered for the 'front line' assault force at Bruneval, their
contribution, albeit important, was eventually limited to a supporting role.

Documented evidence to back up the story of a dummy raid on Ventnor
is conspicuous by its absence among the files at the National Archives on
Biting, and the training which preceded it. The archived documents at Kew
are comprehensive; they include an appendix listing details of the training
programme on a day-by-day basis. At no stage does it mention the Isle of
Wight.[2]

There are preserved local wartime records on the Isle of Wight compiled
by Air Raid Precautions (ARP) officers which might reasonably be expected
to include reference, albeit possibly oblique given the presumed need for
secrecy, to an exercise such as the one described online. In fact, aside from
a report by the Royal Observer Corps, forwarded to the ARP by the police,
of unexplained 'flares' off the island's southern coastal tip in the early hours
of 26 January, there is nothing to suggest a mock assault in the run-up to the
Bruneval raid.[3]

However, from this period, the first two months of 1942, there is at least
one intriguing reference which perhaps should not be overlooked. A book
published in 1979, eighteen years after her death, featured in edited form
the wartime diaries – which originally had filled fifteen exercise books –

of Warwickshire woman Clara Milburn. On Monday, 16 February 1942, Mrs Milburn noted that she had that day received a letter from a friend which told of 'a Nazi landing on the south coast and the seizure of two Home Guards, who were carried off!' Quite apart from her correspondent's evident disregard for the government's widely-issued edict that 'careless talk costs lives,' Clara Milburn's record of this startling (on the face of it, at least) piece of information is fascinating for the light-hearted manner in which she wrote it down. 'That ought to "larn" the H.G. to shoot first!' she added without an apparent trace of concern. Whatever she truly thought of this at the time, her diary made no further reference to it.

Mrs Milburn's Diaries: An Englishwoman's Day-to-Day Reflections 1939–45, edited by Peter Donnelly for London publishers George G. Harrap and Co., offers a particularly revealing take on the war from a home front perspective but poses some tantalising questions. Did Clara Milburn, as her manner suggests, regard and accordingly dismiss her friend's report as just another rumour? Had a mock British raid somehow given rise to the story of a German landing? Was the Isle of Wight involved at all? We are left only with conjecture about this one.

However, it *is* possible to verify the ultimate source of the reported 'dry run' attack on RAF Ventnor. It is taken from an interview with former soldier A.T. Rodway which featured in my book, *The Isle of Wight at War: 1939–45*, published by the Dovecote Press in 1989. Mr Rodway had served in the early stages of the war as a private with No. 2 Special Service Battalion and his recall of the mock raid, as reproduced in the book, has clearly since been summarised for repeated use online. 'The look of absolute amazement on the faces of the air force men and women was truly remarkable. I am sure their thoughts later were, "Thank God it was only an exercise!"' A.C. Rodway had remarked in the interview, a comment the more recent internet version tends to omit.

So why are there no references to a mock attack, or indeed to a Colin Newman, in official records or published works on Operation Biting? In fact, there *was* an officer by the name of Newman in the Special Service Brigade. Augustus 'Gus' Newman, a lieutenant-colonel in the Essex Regiment prior to the war, served with the brigade before assuming command of No. 2 Commando, in which role he led with courageous disregard for his own safety the spectacular amphibious assault in March 1942 on the dry dock at the German-held western French port of St Nazaire. Newman's inspirational leadership of his men deservedly earned him the Victoria Cross.

While most sources insist he was earlier attached to No. 1 Special Service Battalion rather than No. 2, the former Private Rodway clearly identified Gus Newman as his superior officer on the mock raid when recounting his story in 1989, specifically mentioning Newman's later VC award for the St Nazaire mission, but wrongly recalled his first name as Colin. This error was not spotted at the time and has been constantly repeated in the summaries online.

This still leaves the apparent conflict over Newman's involvement in the training for Biting. He was certainly not involved in the raid itself but, if A.C. Rodway was correct in linking the mock assault on Ventnor with preparations for Bruneval, why has this been ignored in the subsequent histories? There is no real answer to this. One possible explanation is that a mock raid on the Isle of Wight site *did* take place, but at an earlier stage in the war, when the special service battalions were still known as such, than the period preceding preparations for the February 1942 operation in France. That it happened we can have little doubt and therefore it does stand as a possible source of confusion with the legendary German raid in 1943, especially in the context of that version of the legend which suggests that, despite the extreme geographical difficulties of access that would have confronted a seaborne enemy force, RAF Ventnor on the top of St Boniface Down was the target for the German raiding party.

The presence and layout of an 'outer minefield' protecting the RAF compound, a highly daunting deterrent for would-be enemy raiders, presumably would have been notified in advance of the mock attack to the British special forces and consequently avoided at all costs! They would surely also have been briefed on the several machine gun posts dotted around the site. It is, in fact, unclear whether there *was* a minefield on St Boniface Down. A wartime site plan of RAF Ventnor, prepared as a secret document for restricted use and not declassified until January 1958, shows the technical compound surrounded by wire fencing but does not indicate the presence of a perimeter minefield. However, the plan is dated November 1944 so cannot be said with certainty to be a true representation of the situation earlier in the war.[4]

If we are to look for firm links between the British raid on Bruneval and the rumoured German counterattack on the Isle of Wight, assuming for the moment that the latter was a reality and the details underpinning the story are fact, these are not difficult to find. The most obvious is that both were launched – entirely in the case of Brunevel, arguably less so in the raid on the island – to uncover secrets of the enemy's radar shield and return home with key pieces of equipment for scientific evaluation. Both achieved this aim. Both involved a firefight. If we adhere to one version of the island's legend, both also involved the taking of prisoners. Before looking more closely at the German raid and considering the likely truth behind it, assessment of the Bruneval assault, its authenticity assured, presents the far simpler task.

With RAF losses in bomber raids against the enemy unacceptably high, intense interest in Germany's radar defences had dominated the thoughts of Britain's military scientists in 1941. Leading the team was the physicist and scientific intelligence expert Reginald (always referred to as R.V.) Jones. At the outbreak of war in September 1939, shortly before his twenty-eighth birthday, he had moved from the Royal Aircraft Establishment at Farnborough, a branch of the Air Ministry, where his time had been largely spent working on ways to safeguard the nation against aerial attack, to a ground-breaking new role in another part of the ministry's domain. Jones had become the first scientist assigned to its intelligence section and was soon appointed Assistant Director of Intelligence (Science), in which post, convinced of German RDF efficiency, he directed the quest for a detailed picture of the radar shield mushrooming along the Channel coast of France.[5]

The RAF's low-level aerial reconnaissance in the autumn of 1941 had clearly revealed the existence of one of the Germans' hitherto secret Würzburg early warning radar stations, which stood in front of a large chateau a short distance inland from a virtually sheer-sided cliff. Germany's principal ground-based gun-laying radar, designed to determine range, azimuth and evaluation of a target for use by both the army and air force, the Wurzburg took its name from the city in northern Bavaria. Developed before the war, it had been in service since 1940 but little was known in Britain about its specific engineering and scientific features.

Jones saw the possibility of a commando-style raid on the isolated site – but was this achievable? Any frontal assault on, and escape from, the site via the cliff would have been a highly risky venture. For this reason, the use of commando forces was ruled out as potentially too costly. However, the photographs obtained from the RAF had also shown, close by, a slope leading down to a small beach. If an airlifted raiding party could surprise the enemy from behind and successfully carry out its mission, the slope offered a means of getting away by sea.

The use of airborne forces had been pioneered by the Red Army in the 1930s and refined with great success by the Germans in the early years of World War Two during the *Blitzkrieg* offensive on Belgium and Holland, and then the assault on Crete in May 1941. The huge potential of sending in soldiers by air had been recognised in Britain and by June 1940 the country's first paratroopers, an initial force of 500 men, had begun training at RAF Ringway near Manchester. At the end of October 1941, this fledgling unit came under the command of newly-promoted Major-General Frederick 'Boy' Browning following his appointment – at the personal behest of Prime Minister Winston Churchill – as head of parachute and airborne troops. In the following month Browning developed the concept by forming the 1st Airborne Division.

Born in 1896, Browning had been educated at Eton and the Royal Military College, Sandhurst, before starting his military service in 1915 as a second lieutenant. Joining the Grenadier Guards, he served with distinction during the First World War and had enjoyed a distinguished and highly-decorated army career. He would later rightly be recalled as the 'father' of Britain's airborne forces, despite his arrival on the scene more than a year after recruitment of the first paratroopers, but initially he faced something of an uphill struggle to prove the worth of a division as yet untested in battle and facing stiff competition for manpower and resources from the more traditional components of the nation's military strength. It says much for his organisational skills (and an impressive list of personal contacts acquired from years of social networking) that he was able to develop the 1st Airborne into a significant, highly capable part of the army.

The division's expansion under Browning saw the evolution of the 1st Parachute Brigade, equipped with two battalions. Training was focussed on having the force ready for action by midsummer 1942. In the event, with parachute training barely completed, the call to arms came much earlier when, with the official backing of Mountbatten at Combined Operations, the brigade was chosen in January of that year for the top-secret special operation against the radar site at Bruneval. Men from one of the two battalions would be needed for the mission. On paper, the logical choice for Operation Biting was the longer established 1st Battalion, which had been in training for more than a year. However, the brigade's CO, Brigadier Richard Gale, had other ideas. Keen to demonstrate that his entire brigade was ready for war at any time, he decided instead that elements of the 2nd Battalion should provide the raiding force.

At the forefront of the assault would be men of the battalion's C Company, formed almost entirely from soldiers who had served previously with famous Scottish regiments, the Black Watch and Cameron Highlanders, together with a smattering of the 'Cockney Jocks' (or 'Piccadilly Allsorts') drawn from the ranks of the London Scottish. The company would be commanded by a tough 29-year-old Cameronian, Major John (widely known as Johnny) Frost.

C Company's role as the operation's ground force was not the army's only contribution to Biting. Engineering expertise was going to be essential if the raiders were to fulfil Jones' objective of dismantling key radar equipment at Bruneval and returning with it to England. This would be provided by a ten-strong detachment of sappers from the 1st Air Troop Royal Engineers under the command of Lieutenant Dennis Vernon. While he could brief them on electronics (and how to avoid electrocuting themselves), Vernon's men would not, of course, come ready equipped with specialised knowledge of state-of-the-art radar apparatus. The raid's planners would clearly need to look elsewhere, beyond the resources of the army, for that.

Placed under the overall command of the Royal Navy's Admiral Sir William 'Bubbles' James, Commander-in-Chief at Portsmouth,[6] Biting would be developed as a multi-service assignment, a classic combined operation involving all three armed forces. Quite apart from the fact that the RAF would be called upon to transport the raiding party to their cross-Channel objective (with the Royal Navy on hand to bring them back home), in the run-up to the operation the army's selected paratroopers and engineers were joined in their training by Flight Sergeant Charles Cox, a man destined to play a central role. Cox had been a cinema projectionist before the war but was now serving with the RAF as a radar operative. Acknowledged as a highly-skilled technician, his responsibility, after landing with the parachuted force, would be to examine the captured Würzburg apparatus on the spot and assess quickly which parts of it the engineers should attempt to plunder for analysis back in the UK.

Technical expertise was one thing. Flying to France in what was certain to be uncomfortably cramped conditions and dropping unseen to the ground in darkness by parachute was quite another, as indeed was travelling home by sea. Cox had never set foot in either a plane or a ship! He was detailed to assist with training Vernon and some of his sappers in the rudiments of radar technology so that, should he become incapacitated during the assault, at least a few of the engineers might still be able to recognise and grab something useful to carry back with them.

In a sense, Cox was something of a fall guy, vital to the success of the operation but a man whose capture by the enemy, if the worst came to the worst, could – just about – be risked. He was certainly well versed in RDF technology, but did not possess the specialist knowledge of British radar development that would render him an unacceptable security gamble in the hands of German interrogators. So Cox would land with the raiding force, while the mission's ultimate expert in the field, the bespectacled scientist Don Preist (often misspelt as Priest) from the Telecommunications Research Establishment in Dorset, would not be risked in the heat of battle. Instead, he would travel as the force's technical adviser to Bruneval with the naval flotilla entrusted with bringing the Biting raiders home and would only be allowed ashore if Major Frost's men succeeded in completely clearing the target area of enemy forces.

Given the temporary RAF rank of flight lieutenant, Preist's immediate return to England was essential. It was the life of Flight Sergeant Charles Cox which would be firmly on the line at Bruneval. Indeed, raid folklore suggests C Company were under orders to shoot Cox if he fell into German hands to prevent him revealing sensitive information on the British radar deterrent, although few sources now give any credence to the story, dismissing as a myth.

If any of this led to sleepless nights for Cox, few of Johnny Frost's officers and men, and the sappers in training with them, would have been overly anxious as their preparations began. Biting was a top secret operation. It was essential the enemy did not get to hear about it. To limit the potential for such a calamity, knowledge of the planned raid and its objectives, the real reason the men were being prepared for action, was strictly restricted on a 'need to know' basis. Major Frost, initially in the dark himself, was sworn to secrecy when he learnt the truth. He and the others in the 'know' had to keep it to themselves. The assembled force trained in the belief they had been selected to stage an exercise for the War Cabinet in order to demonstrate techniques and capabilities for raiding a headquarters building behind enemy lines. Everything was done to disguise the true nature of the men's mission. As part of this, they were allocated quarters at Tilshead camp, a training base on Salisbury Plain used by another of Britain's fledgling airborne forces, the Glider Pilot Regiment, which had only just become active.

Initially absent – he was in the north of England completing the statutory number of jumps required for his parachutist's wings, an objective delayed by an injury sustained on his first jump – Frost would have had mixed feelings on receiving news of how his men's transfer to Tilshead had gone. The allotted barracks there were mud-splattered, draughty and uncomfortable; the camp outside 'an ugly, dirty dump', as author Taylor Downing put it in *Night Raid: The true story of the first victorious British para raid of WWII*, his comprehensive 2013 review of the Bruneval mission for the Little, Brown Book Group in London. As for Major Frost's own assessment of the accommodation, according to George Millar he summarily denounced Tilshead camp as 'a miserable hole'. However, as intended, the paras' arrival on Salisbury Plain as 'just another unit' had provoked barely a spark of interest.

There was nothing uninteresting in the arrival on the scene of a new recruit for the raiding force. Major Frost was initially surprised and more than a little unsettled when, on 8 February 1942, he met for the first time a young man from the Pioneer Corps, introduced to him simply as 'Private Newman'. Clearly a good soldier, with admirable determination and enthusiasm, 'Newman' brought something else to the party, a quality otherwise lacking in the make-up of the Biting force; he could speak fluent

German. Should the raiders succeed in capturing members of the enemy's troops guarding the radar site or, as planned, one of the radar operatives, the ability to communicate quickly and easily with them was seen as a prized asset.

Frost could see the wisdom of that but seriously questioned the raid planners' choice of interpreter. 'Not only could Private Newman speak German, but he *was* German,' wrote Downing in his 2011 book, adding that the private's real identity was Peter Nagel, a 25-year-old Berlin-born Jew who had escaped Nazi Germany before the war and had served with the British Army since March 1940. His credentials were sound but Frost's initial scepticism was understandable for a man charged with leading such a high-risk mission. Frost was worried. Had the enemy learnt of the operation? Was his new recruit a plant? It would need the personal assurances of Mountbatten to convince the major that taking 'Private Newman' was a safe bet. And so it proved. 'His knowledge of the German language and of the psychology of Germans proved of great assistance,' General Browning would later observe in a post-raid report.[7]

Thus, we *do* have a soldier with the surname of Newman, albeit in this case an alias, in the Bruneval story. He had an inferior status and served in a wholly different unit of the British Army – but has Operation Biting's 'Private Newman' in some way been conflated with Gus Newman whose name, albeit incorrectly recalled, features prominently in the tale of a mock raid on RAF Ventnor? It might help to explain why the link between the two events has persisted. On the face of it, this seems a doubtful proposition. Coincidence appears far more likely.

As for the suggested mock raid itself, a variety of dress rehearsals, as might be expected, were certainly organised for Biting. In his succinct, highly readable, 2010 account of the mission, *The Bruneval Rail: Operation Biting 1942*, commissioned by Oxford-based Osprey Publishing, military historian Ken Ford told of one practice exercise soon after the paras' arrival at Tilshead camp, but to take part in this, Major Frost's force was not even required to leave Wiltshire, let alone cross the Solent to 'attack' RAF Ventnor's radar. The exercise, wrote Ford, was 'organised on a speedily selected area of high ground near Alton Priors, close to the Kennet and Avon Canal ... the high ground represented the cliffs at Bruneval and the canal was the sea.'

The exercise called for C Company to be split into a number of sections, each with a specific task. Airborne drops did not feature. 'The purpose of the exercise was to train for the ground operations of the eventual raid,' explained Ford, adding that it went very well, with all groups satisfactorily fulfilling their allotted tasks.

Airborne drops were, of course, an essential part of the preparations for Biting, and it wasn't just the raiding party who were being prepared in the early months of 1942 for a parachuted descent into enemy territory. The RAF, too, was honing its own principal contribution to the mission – taking the paras and those going with them on the cross-Channel flight to France. Chosen for the task, which would necessitate a tricky low-altitude approach to the Normandy coastline, were men of No. 51 Squadron, equipped with a fleet of the RAF's 'flying barn doors'!

This was perhaps one of the less strident tags applied colloquially to the Armstrong Whitworth A.W. 38 Whitley aircraft. 'Ugly,' 'matronly' and 'slow' were among the other more printable alternatives! The twin-engine Whitley had entered the war as the oldest of Britain's three medium bomber types, along with the Wellington and the Hampden. Although 51 Squadron had been allocated the Mark V version of the Whitley, by 1942, as work to convert a dozen for their role in Operation Biting gathered momentum, they were all but obsolete.

As a conveyance for parachutists, the Whitley left a lot to be desired. In addition to an RAF crew of five (the captain, two observers, an air gunner and a wireless operator) plus space for equipment, there was just enough room to squeeze in ten members of the raiding force per plane. This troop complement reflected the technical necessity of the period for parachutists to drop in 'sticks' of ten. Seating would be a luxury denied to them. The floor of the narrow fuselage would have to suffice – backs against one side; feet against the other. The sole means provided for leaving the aircraft above the target area was via a circular trapdoor cut into the floor, risking serious injury, particularly to the head, if the exit was not performed correctly. Coupled with the Whitley's shortcomings was 51 Squadron's lack of experience in dropping men rather than bombs from their aircraft. The squadron boasted a fine record in extensive night bombing operations, but this was a wholly unaccustomed new role.

If the Whitleys were a worry to Frost and his men, 51 Squadron's CO was anything but. Wing-Commander Charles 'Pick' Pickard, the man who would lead Biting's RAF component, was both popular – universally so – and inspirational. At the age of just 26, he was also a celebrity. Pickard, 'tall, fair-headed and pipe-smoking,' according to George Millar, had played a leading role in the 1941 propaganda film, *Target for Tonight*, featuring as the pilot of *F for Freddie*, a Wellington bomber. 'Everybody liked him,' wrote Millar, 'whether he was hanging by his feet from a rafter in the mess bar, proving that he could drink a pint of beer upside-down, or whether he was landing a single-engine Lysander in a dark field in the occupied zone of France.' When Frost's men travelled from Tilshead for an introductory meeting with 51 Squadron at Thruxton aerodrome, they were immediately won over by Pickard, truly one of the RAF's most colourful personalities of the war.

From Tilshead, the insignia from their uniforms removed for security reasons, Frost's force travelled by train on 9 February to Scotland. Travelling separately to the same destination were a number of men from No. 12 (Irish and Welsh) Commando, chosen for a key role in support of the paratroopers and engineers. In icy conditions, raid preparations now took on a wholly different character as C Company and, to quote George Millar, their 'appendages,' arrived on the northwest coast at Inverary, the old garrison town on the north bank of the narrow waters of Loch Fyne, the longest of the Scottish sea lochs. The paras were there to undergo specialised training in the art of embarking at night by landing craft, as they would need to do from Bruneval following the raid. For their part, the commandos would be detailed to provide covering fire from the landing craft. It was time to involve the Royal Navy.

By way of contrast with the markedly less than salubrious accommodation they had been forced to endure at Tilshead, Frost's men now found themselves housed in comparative luxury aboard HMS *Prins Albert*, an impressively capacious landing ship which had begun life in 1937 as a Belgian passenger vessel, requisitioned and converted for her new use by the Royal Navy after the fall of Belgium in 1940. She was capable of accommodating thirty-nine army officers and 300 other ranks in addition to a carrying capacity of eight assault landing craft (LCA), widely manufactured in the UK to ferry troops from landing ships to enemy-held shores..

The latter part of the plan for Biting was to evacuate the raiding force from the beach at Bruneval aboard six of the *Prins Albert's* LCA following the landing crafts' arrival offshore, accompanied by a small fleet of motor gun boats (MGB), from their mother ship, anchored further out from the French coast. As the *Prins Albert* – something of a sitting duck, considering her size, in such a vulnerable position – returned to England, the LCA would move in to the beach once they had received a signal from Major Frost's men that they were ready to depart. From the LCA, the raiding force would be transferred to the gun boats which, with the landing craft in tow, would then carry the men and, hopefully, the captured radar components home to Portsmouth. Placed in charge of naval operations was Commander Frederick (usually known as F.N.) Cook, of the Royal Australian Navy. A few days short of his thirty-seventh birthday, Cook was an excellent choice given his role since the end of 1940 in command of HMS *Tormentor*, Combined Operations' Warsash training base at the mouth of the River Hamble on the Hampshire coast, a unit specialising in the handling of landing craft.

As his men settled in to their new quarters aboard the *Prins Albert*, Frost had still to tell them the truth about the upcoming raid – the cover story remained intact – but the nature and intensity of the training on Loch Fyne, and the identity of the ship itself, must strongly have nudged the paras towards a realisation that they were being prepared for something more pressing and considerably more important than a mere demonstration of capability for the PM.

It was certainly no easy ride. Despite the company's evident enjoyment at the chance to spend time 'messing about in boats,' things did not go well operationally in Scotland. The beaches were strewn with rocks – problematic enough for embarkation in daylight; difficult in the extreme at night and decidedly hazardous if the weather should suddenly turn foul. George Millar noted:

'And there was always that phenomenon, the tide. Whether it was flowing or ebbing, always it seemed to be wrong for what they wanted to do. Then, too, the naval crews seemed to have the greatest difficulty in finding the dark figures on the darker shores. They never appeared to be able to distinguish flashlight signals and they often missed coloured Very lights.'

Night-time embarkation was threatening to prove an obstacle too far for C Company. Johnny Frost was growing ever more uneasy at this highly unsatisfactory state of affairs.

So it was possibly while trying to convince himself 'it'll be alright on the night' that he and his men were summoned from an exercise ashore back to the *Prins Albert*. Admiral Mountbatten was aboard; their presence was urgently required. Finally, it was time to reveal to all involved the real purpose of their presence on Loch Fyne; a dress rehearsal for a small-scale, yet highly significant, combined operation against the enemy. If some of the paras had guessed as much, the news came as a complete surprise to the naval complement who listened to the admiral. Until then they had no idea their army guests were parachutists and no inkling that they themselves would be sailing on the *Prins Albert* with a crucial role to play in the upcoming mission. Mountbatten stressed the importance of co-operation between the two military services and with the RAF, whose job, he told them, would be to fly the raiders to France.

Major Frost's enlightened force left the tricky training waters of Inverary the next morning. The *Prins Albert* took them down the loch and then to the coastal town of Gourock. From there, as the landing ship adopted a southwards course en route for Portsmouth, the paras and sappers began the long journey by rail back to Salisbury Plain and the unwelcoming barracks at Tilshead, arriving there on 14 February. On the following day, loaded with the equipment they would need for the real thing, the entire force linked up with 51 Squadron for a practice drop from the Whitleys close to Major-General Browning's Wiltshire HQ at Sycamore House, near Figheldean. The general expressed his satisfaction with the progress he felt sure was being made. Frost, on the other hand, would later describe this rehearsal drop as 'a shambles'.

His mood was far from lightened when the force headed for the Dorset coast at Redcliff Point, east of Weymouth, on 16 February in a bid to iron out with the Royal Navy the difficulties experienced in Scotland with night-time embarkation. Frustratingly, this was thwarted by bad weather; the exercise was abandoned. Thoughts now turned to a full-scale night rehearsal the following day, with plans for both the navy and air force to rehearse their roles with C Company. Offering a coastal break in the chalk hills of the Purbeck Ridge, the small bay and beach at Arish Mell, a short distance west of Lulworth Cove, was a pretty good location for it, or would have been had the weather not once again intervened to spoil the show.

On paper, this should have been the most complete practice in the training process. The plan was for the raiding force to be taken overland to an assembly area, as if they had arrived by air, while the Whitleys of 51 Squadron dropped parachuted containers into the pre-designated zone. 'The troops would rendezvous with their equipment, carry out their set tasks and then withdraw by sea on landing craft,' wrote Ken Ford. Other sources record that, to add a further layer of authenticity, men dressed in captured German uniforms were to represent the enemy.

Sadly, it all went wrong. 'Unfortunately,' added Ford in describing the exercise, 'the weather turned bad at the last minute and the landing craft could not arrive. The aircraft dropped their containers wide of their mark and Frost's company went to the wrong place.' In fact, they found themselves in the midst of a minefield, part of the defences against feared German invasion, several miles from where they should have been. 'They were lucky to get out without any casualties,' observed Taylor Downing in his account. Major Frost's later summation of the Arish Mell exercise was no doubt aptly expressed. It was, he said, 'a disaster'.

On the following evening they tried again. The outcome was much the same, poor weather once more preventing the landing craft's arrival at Arish Mell. Frustrated, the raiding force returned on 19 February to Tilshead camp and learnt, very probably to collective dismay, that an initial attempt on the operation itself, determined by a study of weather projections and tidal conditions, was scheduled to take place in just five days' time, on the night of Tuesday, 24th.

RAF preparations had been complex. For the men of 51 Squadron, the run-up to Biting represented a steep learning curve far in excess of mastering the art of delivering parachutists instead of bombs to a target area via practice missions with dummies. Raid historians also tell of the need to perfect map-reading at low altitudes and rehearse timed cross-country flights with low approaches.in advance of dress rehearsals with the parachutists. By this time the bomb-release mechanism on the Whitleys had been modified to allow the automatic release of equipment containers at the same time as the parachutists, an essential pre-requisite to success.

In the wider context, the air force had a vital additional role to play. Deception was at the heart of it; a bid to allay German suspicions in the Le Havre area at the sudden appearance of British bombers flying in over the Normandy coast at low altitude. As the countdown to the Bruneval mission gathered pace, a succession of low-level overnight raids were mounted by aircraft from No. 4 Group Bomber Command (of which 51 Squadron formed part) to accustom the enemy to such tactics, lead them to think the Biting mission was just another bombing raid and dissuade them from any notion that Bruneval's radar installation was under threat. A diversionary raid on the night of the operation would extend the deception a stage further. RAF Fighter Command would also play its part, with No. 11 Group set to provide Spitfire cover for the raiding force once daybreak had arrived on its seaborne return from France.

The final days of preparation for all concerned with Operation Biting were devoted largely to fine-tuning the 'small print' of the mission masterplan – the provision of special clothing, the collection and testing of equipment, the packing of containers – but the opportunity was also taken for Frost's men to rehearse attacks on pillbox defences and practice crossing barbed wire obstacles. Most importantly, with landing craft embarkation still a thorny issue, a final attempt at resolving this key aspect was urgently needed. Commander Cook, for one, insisted on it.

Accordingly, army and navy raid personnel gathered in Hampshire on 20 February for a practice in Southampton Water, close to Cook's naval shore base at HMS *Tormentor*. By all accounts, this was the closest the training for Biting ever came to the Isle of Wight, a few miles to the south across the Solent. Almost predictably, it was again beset by frustration. More bad weather, so often the scourge of mission training, delayed the exercise until the night of Sunday, 22 February, a mere two days before the planned initial date for the raid itself.

This time the weather was favourable and visibility clear, as were inter-service communications. But the navy had miscalculated the tides. Major Frost's men could only watch in dismay as the landing craft were forced to beach about sixty yards out. Frost was left with little choice. Instructing his men to leave their weapons behind to avoid salt water damage, he then ordered them to wade out into the bitterly cold sea in order to reach the boats.

Taylor Downing described the fiasco that followed:

'They waded out into the dark, forbidding and frozen sea until the water was three feet deep, but they still had not reached the landing craft. As they got further out the sea got even deeper and began to lap over their thighs. Some of the men almost froze with cold and cramp. And when they reached the landing craft the vessels were once again caught on the tide and would not budge. The men had to wade back ashore and the exercise was abandoned.'

The last chance to perfect the plan for evacuating Bruneval was lost in the mud.

Given this series of setbacks, it was a blessing that Biting's planners were able to provide the raiders with first-rate Intelligence to smooth their way. Preparations had been greatly helped by the good work of the French Resistance, who had reconnoitred the radar site and its defences, and by the use of scale models of the site and its environs made by the RAF's Central Interpretation Unit at Medenham, Buckinghamshire, using the excellent set of photographs obtained from aerial reconnaissance. Together, this was to prove of immense value.

Mirroring the organisational set-up in the latter stages of training, C Company and its attendant specialists, a total of 120 men, were to be divided into three main groups for the assault, with further sub-divisions into small parties allotted specific tasks within their group's overall objectives. As befits the patriotic, daredevil nature of the mission, the various components of the main paratrooper force were each given the name of a renowned British naval hero. Nelson, Drake, Hardy, Jellicoe and Rodney were the five illustrious names chosen.

Major General Robert Laycock in 1943, the year he was appointed Chief of Combined Operations. Did the 'absolutely splendid' German commando raid he lauded refer to the Isle of Wight landing? (*Imperial War Museum*)

Major General Robert Laycock, Chief of Combined Operations, inspects Royal Marine Commandos shortly before D-Day in 1944. Two years later he was full of praise for a German commando raid. (*Imperial War Museum*)

The classic RAF aerial reconnaissance photograph of the Germans' Wurzburg radar site (in front of chateau) at Bruneval, Normandy, scene of the famous 1942 British raid. Was the Isle of Wight landing in 1943 a tit-for-tat mission? (*Imperial War Museum*)

With Major Johnny Frost on the bridge (second left), a Royal Navy MTB brings men of C Company, 2nd Battalion Parachute Regiment into Portsmouth Harbour on the morning after the successful raid on Bruneval in February 1942. (*Imperial War Museum*)

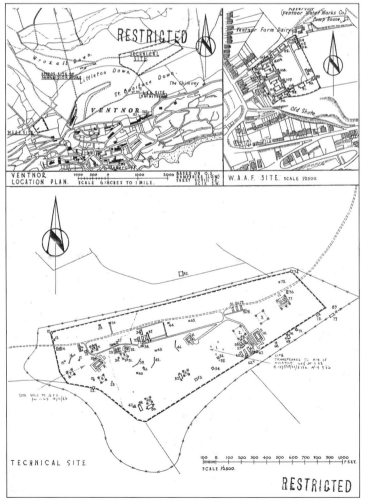

Wartime site plan of RAF Ventnor, principal radar station on the Isle of Wight and the target for a mock assault by British special forces in training – but a target too far for the legendary German raiders. (*Author's collection*)

The former site of RAF Ventnor on St Boniface Down survives today as a radar station, though in greatly modified form and now under civil control. As this picture shows, a reminder of its former military use has been erected by Ventnor & District Local History Society. (*Matt Searle*)

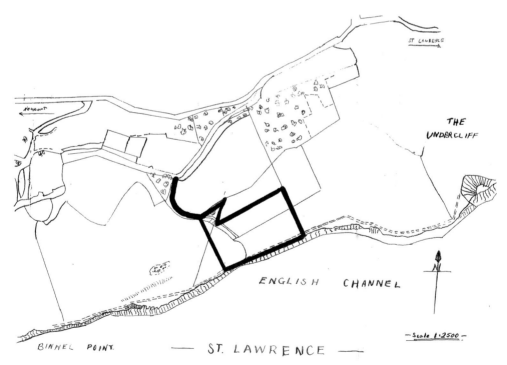

A contemporary map of the St Lawrence area with the outline of the wartime radar site clearly marked. Access from Woolverton Road, leading to the remainder of the local road network was via the semi-circular farm track shown. (*Sam Twining*)

The German target.
A photograph of
Woody Bay with the
radar pylons of RAF
St Lawrence on the
clifftop. While taken
shortly after the war,
this picture illustrates
the relatively shallow
profile of the cliffs
beneath the radar
station. (*Francis Frith*)

Close-up image of the two 105-
foot wooden radar masts at RAF
St Lawrence, a photograph from
the 1945 victory souvenir edition
of *Radar Bulletin* magazine (which
did not actually identify the site).
(*Author's collection*)

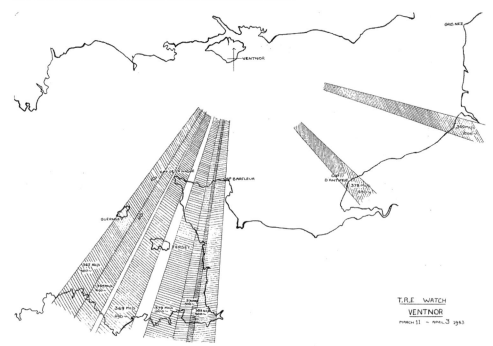

Official diagrammatic map of the watch for enemy signals intelligence carried out by the
Telecommunications Research Establishment from RAF Ventnor in March and April 1943, a matter
of months before the Germans are believed to have landed on the Isle of Wight. (*National Archives*)

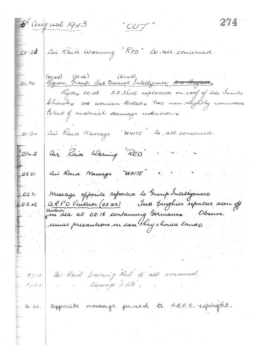

01.22	Air Raid Warning "RED"
01.23	ARPO Ventnor (01.23) Plane reported down, now confirmed as flares
01.33	Air Raid Message "WHITE"
01.32	ARPO Ryde (01.40) 2 minor casualties. Mr. Lofts, Mr. Matthews attended by local doctors. Object striking Church established as U.P. Shell
01.40	Air Raid Warning "RED"
02.20	Air Raid Message "WHITE"
02.30	A.R.P.O. Newport (02.31) Special Report. Police report 2 dinghies full of Germans in sea off Ventnor. Seen at 02.18/160. (Reported to Police through Navy)
02.40	ARPO Ventnor (02.45) N.F.S. Report fire near Pylons at Ventnor. 2 Pumps are dealing with it.
07.09	Air Raid Warning Red.
07.24	" " Message White
13.46	SW. Sub District. (16.30) The following practical SHOOTING is intended 2146 hrs 16 Aug 43 CLIFF END. + 19 "

01.23	Air Raid Warning "RED" to all concerned.
01.30	(0140) (01.46) (01.40) Region, Group, Sub District Intelligence. Ryde, 00.18 A.A. Shell exploded on roof of All Saints Church. One woman killed. Two men slightly wounded. Extent of material damage unknown.
01.34	Air Raid Message "WHITE" to all concerned.
01.42	Air Raid Warning "RED" " "
02.21	Air Raid Message "WHITE" " "
02.31	Message opposite reported to Group Intelligence
02.42	ARPO Ventnor (02.42) Two dinghies reported seen off Ventnor in sea at 02.18 containing Germans. Observe usual precautions in case they should land.
07.10	Air Raid Warning Red to all concerned.
07.22	" " Message White
16.30	Opposite message passed to A.R.P.O. Isle of Wight.

The dramatic incoming message (enhanced text) made in the Isle of Wight ARP record book at 2.30 on the morning of 16 August 1943 of 'two dinghies full of Germans in sea off Ventnor coast' – believed to be the only accessible British documentation of the German landing. (*Isle of Wight Record Office*)

The ARP's outward message made at 2.42 from its Newport headquarters soon after receiving reports of the German presence, instructing wardens to 'observe usual precautions in case they should land'. (*Isle of Wight Record Office*)

A young Alfred Lomnitz in Germany before he changed his surname to Laurence following his exposure to Nazi brutality in Dachau and Sachsenhausen concentration camps during the 1930s. (*Geoffrey Laurence*)

Alfred Laurence (second right, bottom row) during his wartime service with the US Army which eventually returned him to the location of his pre-war Nazi captivity in Dachau and led to his role in bringing the camp's war criminals to justice. (*Geoffrey Laurence*)

Dr Alfred Laurence in later life – a man with an extraordinary past who played a pivotal role in pursuing the truth behind the long-rumoured German landing on the south coast of the Isle of Wight. (*Geoffrey Laurence*)

Dr Dietrich Andernacht, first-hand witness to the 1943 German landing on the Isle of Wight, a raid he actually took part in, is pictured in later life as a highly-respected historian and archivist in Frankfurt. (*Institut für Stadtgeschichte Karmeliterkloster, Frankfurt am Main*)

Gareth Sprack, the Isle of Wight-based military historian whose chance 1981 encounter in France with a former German serviceman provided further first-hand evidence of a mid-war enemy raid on St Lawrence radar station. (*Gareth Sprack*)

German-born Professor Carl Prausnitz, the renowned physician who served as a Ventnor GP between 1935 and 1963. Did he discover medical records relating to the German raid and was then silenced by high authority when he sought further information? (*Southampton Medical Journal*)

Woody Bay, St Lawrence, in 2016. This picture, looking eastwards from the rocky beach, shows how little has changed since World War Two and emphasises the less than daunting climb to the radar station (further left) which would have faced a German raiding party. There would have been no need for the Germans to scale the high ground to the east (right) of the bay. The shallower cliff to the west (left) presented a far easier ascent. (*Matt Searle*)

Relics of the wartime radar station at St Lawrence were still in situ when this picture was taken in 2015 of the former mound-covered standby set-house. Much of the surrounding ground had been cleared of vegetation as plans to convert this part of the site for residential use progressed. (*Matt Searle*)

With the English Channel in the background, this 2015 view shows part of the semi-buried remains of RAF St Lawrence's standby set-house which formerly accommodated the diesel generator providing power to the site in the event of electrical failure. (*Matt Searle*)

A pair of distinctive seven-sided 'Handcraft huts,' further relics of RAF St Lawrence's wartime past, survived among the trees – complete with new doors – when this picture was taken in 2015. (*Matt Searle*)

A quartet of surviving aerial mast bases close to the cliff edge above the English Channel at the former RAF St Lawrence in 2016. Transmitter and receiver blocks were located immediately behind their respective wooden masts, covered in mounds of earth still evident today. (*Matt Searle*)

Nelson comprised all forty men in the first main group – three light attack sections, each of them ten-strong, under 2nd Lieutenant Euan Charteris and a ten-man heavy section led by Captain John Ross, Major Frost's second-in-command. Charteris and his men were assigned the particularly vital role of capturing and holding the beach, which was protected by fixed enemy positions, earmarked for the raiding force's withdrawal by sea. Meanwhile, Ross's heavy section would provide rearguard cover for the Charteris-led contingent and block the road leading to the beach from Bruneval village, assisted by two of the Royal Engineers sappers with anti-tank mines. It would then be Nelson's job to signal to the waiting naval force offshore that the way had been cleared for the landing craft to come in for the planned exit.

The second main grouping combined three of the named sections, ten men apiece, together with Charles Cox and his engineer support. Drake, led by Lieutenant Peter Naumoff, was tasked with containing enemy personnel, a combination of coast defence troops and Luftwaffe, housed in a group of buildings to the north of the chateau which stood behind the Wurzburg apparatus, limiting an obviously serious potential menace to the success of the mission. The initial objective for Hardy, under the direct command of Frost, was to capture the chateau, expected to be occupied by German military, and then provide cover for Cox and his sappers while they dismantled the radar, reinforcing a further section of paratroopers – Jellicoe, under Lieutenant Peter Young – whose job was to protect the engineers from the start.

Last to be dropped would be the third group, the forty men of Rodney section, led by 2nd Lieutenant John Timothy, who would move immediately to the east of the attack zone to hold off any major enemy interference to the landward side. Timothy's men would also act as a mobile reserve, as required, and would then provide the rearguard during the evacuation phase. Although Cox and the small team of engineers with him would be left with precious little time if he was to bring the secrets of the Würzburg back home, Biting was a well-conceived plan.

But no amount of planning could outwit the forces of nature. Poor weather intervened, delaying the assault for several days until, finally, the 'all-clear' was given on the night of Friday, 27 February for the daring operation to proceed. How much of a bite could Biting deliver?

The raid was launched from the new RAF airfield at Thruxton, a few miles west of Andover in Hampshire. The first of the twelve aircraft, painted black to decrease the possibility of detection in the night sky, took off at 5.30 in the evening; the last was in the air at 5.45. The men of the raiding force were uncomfortably crammed together in the bellies of the Whitleys. As they passed round mugs of tea, generously laced with rum, any attempt at nervous conversation was lost to the roar of their aircraft's engines. However, according to one popular television documentary devoted to the famous raid, Charles Cox 'sang lustily above the din'.

It seems he was not the only one. In a post-raid interview for the Reuters news agency, Major Frost commented: 'On the way across in the planes, you would never have thought it was an operational flight. It was more like a joy ride. Every machine, I think, had its own concert party!'

Snow carpeted Normandy's coastal countryside as the raiders closed in on their drop zone. And then it was time to go. 'It was by no means as frightening as everybody had expected,' added Frost in his interview. 'You sat at the hole, looked down and saw a few tracer bullets go past below – and jumped.' For Cox, his parachuted descent was a revelation. He would later recall that, as he jumped from the Whitley, he was able to recognise the terrain below as identical to the maps, photographs and scale models studied so carefully during training, a huge testament to the reconnaissance and interpretive work which had been carried out beforehand. The Intelligence had been superb. As the Whitleys departed, it was otherwise completely quiet. The snow provided a soft landing. The omens were good for Operation Biting.

Both Major Frost and Captain Ross would later heap praise on the RAF crews for their precision delivery of the vast majority of the force to the target area. 'They put us down ten yards from where we wanted to be,' said Ross, 'and within two minutes of leaving the planes the troops were armed, organised and ready to fight.' However, there was an exception to this.

Wing-Commander Pickard's leading Whitley and the aircraft immediately behind it had been caught in German flak near the drop zone and in the confusion both had mistaken their landmarks. As a result, the parachutists they were carrying, half the group charged with eliminating the enemy's beach defences from the rear, had floated down in the Val aux Chais, well south of Bruneval village and their intended drop point. 'A nasty moment,' the young officer leading the twenty-strong group, 2nd Lieutenant Charteris, would later comment. Charteris, however, was not a man easily thwarted. Rapidly assessing the situation, he led his party across the snowbound landscape, bypassing the village en route to their designated drop zone. It was risky and, unsurprisingly, Charteris and his men ran into a German patrol. This first encounter with the enemy ended successfully and, battle-hardened, the paras were soon in place.

Major Frost would later single out Charteris, at just twenty the youngest officer in the force, as 'the real hero' of the raid. Charteris himself, recalling his reaction to landing in completely unfamiliar territory, remarked:

> 'I don't think there's any feeling quite so unpleasant as suddenly finding
> yourself in enemy territory and not knowing where you are ... but then
> I saw another plane [one of the later waves of arriving Whitleys] going
> along low down and I knew in which direction to go, and after a while
> I saw the lighthouse. Then everything was all right.'

Meanwhile, encumbered with the trolleys they were later to use to transport the captured radar equipment, Cox, Vernon's group of engineers and the paras, led by Lieutenant Young, assigned to defend them, successfully negotiated a series of barbed wire obstacles to close in on the Würzburg. As they did so, Johnny Frost and his contingent crept towards the chateau behind it. On reaching the building, he blew a whistle, as planned, to trigger a fierce assault, his men bursting into the chateau's ground floor accommodation, showering it with hand grenades and rapid fire from their Sten submachine guns. In the event, this was not the difficult task it might have been. Surprisingly, the chateau's lower floor appeared to be deserted.

However, as tracer fire pierced the cold night air outside, it was obvious the raiders' presence in the area had been rumbled by the Germans and, from upstairs in the chateau, the sound of gunfire could be discerned above the din. Frost's men rushed up the stairs. There they discovered a solitary German, firing down at Young's party at the radar site. The man stood no chance. He was immediately killed in a burst of Sten gun fire. Nobody else was found in the building and it fell silent. Outside, it was a different story, the startled yells of German defenders combining with rasping bursts of automatic gunfire to create an angry cacophony of noise.

It was clear to Frost that the German fire was directed at the radar site, though not as yet with any degree of accuracy. With the chateau secure, he was able to send in some of his party to reinforce the men defending Cox and the sappers as they defied a ferocious hail of bullets above their heads from the automatic guns while battling to get to grips with the inner workings of the Würzburg, Precision removal of key components was impossible under such conditions. Finesse was abandoned, substituted by brute force. It was a case of tear off and rip out. To make it clearer for the scientists back home to understand how the radar apparatus functioned, flash photography was used as the parts were being removed. Inevitably, this was greeted by an even greater ferocity of fire from the wooded area to the southeast of the radar site.

Major Frost realised the situation was far too hazardous to remain in position for any length of time. After ten minutes, he ordered the force to depart with its booty for the beach. That in itself was fraught with danger. The beach had yet to be made safe for the raiders' withdrawal by sea; the German fortress there was still resisting Euan Charteris and his party. At one stage, the defenders resorted to subterfuge, one of them calling out in perfect English, 'The boats are here,' in the hope of misleading the raiders into believing the shout had come from a Royal Navy officer and encouraging them to chance a run for the beach under machine gun fire. It was a clever ruse, yet one doomed to failure. The Germans were eventually subdued. However, a major problem remained for the British force. There was no sign of the Royal Navy.

They had been delayed by the presence in the area of enemy E-boats. As Nelson group repeatedly signalled through the mist to the naval flotilla with lamps and Very lights, Commander Cook had no option other than to wait for the coast to clear. Just as Frost was preparing to fend off an enemy counterattack, the landing craft appeared through the gloom – in the nick pf time. 'God bless the ruddy Royal Navy, sir!' a relieved signaller called out to him.

He may have had reason, temporarily at least, to reconsider when the commandos embedded with the approaching naval force began firing at figures on the clifftop in the mistaken belief that they were German soldiers attempting to block the raiders' withdrawal. In fact, some of Frost's own men were still there as they waited to repel the enemy's anticipated counter measures. On the beach pandemonium threatened. One of the six landing craft was hastily loaded with men wounded in the raid and the captured radar equipment, leaving the remainder of the retreating party to compete for limited space, crammed unceremoniously into the other five boats. In the confusion, three of the paras' signallers were left behind as the landing craft swung out to sea, the multiple embarkation training woes consigned largely to history. The gunfire ashore, a virtually constant feature for the past two hours, soon fell quiet.

On reaching deeper water, the raiders were safely transferred to Commander Cook's naval gunboats for the journey home, with the landing craft in tow. As the flotilla set course for Portsmouth, the casualties could be assessed. Two soldiers, Privates McIntyre and Scott, had been killed, their bodies unavoidably left behind in France, eight returned as injury victims and a further six had been captured (though, happily, all would survive the war). According to captured German records, five of their number (two army; three air force) had died in the fighting, two were wounded and a further five were listed as missing, three of whom – including one of the Luftwaffe's Würzburg, operators – had been taken captive. However, statistics for the German casualties vary enormously. In his 1942 raid assessment, now preserved at the National Archives,[8] General Browning claimed 'a minimum of forty killed' among the personnel defending the radar site, in sharp contrast to the official German records.

To fend off any last-ditch attempt by the Luftwaffe to thwart the force's safe return, just as dawn was breaking the flotilla was met and escorted towards home waters by a squadron of Spitfires. In the event, the German air force failed to put in an appearance and the escort for the final leg of the journey was provided by Royal Navy destroyers. As if to emphasise the importance of this extraordinary raid to future strategy and morale in equal measure, a triumphant rendition of *Rule Britannia* blared defiantly from the loudspeakers of the warships.

From the deck of his gunboat, Johnny Frost surveyed the scene as the flotilla neared the haven of Portsmouth Harbour. After the weeks of secrecy and stealth which had underpinned the planning for Biting, this loudly triumphal return must have seemed a strange experience for the man who had so brilliantly led the paras' intrepid mission, but at the same time, a hugely satisfying one. Frost had been advised by Flight Sergeant Cox that he and his team had succeeded in bringing home just about everything needed for a proper evaluation of the Würzburg, an assessment echoed by Biting's scientific expert Donald Preist, who had remained at sea throughout. The pair's declared admiration for the fine workmanship which characterised the German radar rig evidently matched their delight in capturing it at Bruneval. Amid a succession of military setbacks for Britain, this was truly an all-round success to savour.

The scientists in particular had a field day. R.V. Jones and then the boffins at the Telecommunications Research Establishment were able to carry out a revelatory analysis of the Würzburg. At their Worth Matravers base in Dorset, the TRE successfully undertook a rebuild of the radar using the dismantled parts. They deduced a great deal about the limits to which the radar could be tuned and, crucially, confirmed that it possessed no built-in counter to jamming. Later, meticulous examination by Jones of the works numbers on the Würzburg's replacement components allowed him to calculate that the Germans were deploying around one hundred of these radars every month. It was clear from this that, while Bruneval's had been an early model, the technology used in later versions was basically the same.[9, 10]

Several of the operation's key players were rewarded with medals. Among the nineteen decorations announced in May 1942, both Major Frost and the enterprising Lieutenant Charteris received the Military Cross (MC) with Flight Sergeant Cox, whose contribution according to General Browning's raid analysis was 'excellent throughout', one of three men in the raiding force awarded the Military Medal (MM). For his leadership of the naval force, Commander Cook received the Distinguished Service Cross (DSC).[11] Two further DSCs were awarded and two men received the Distinguished Service Medal (DSM), with another nine mentioned in despatches. The RAF's already highly decorated Wing-Commander Pickard subsequently received a bar to the Distinguished Service Order (DSO) he had received in 1941.

An early German response to Operation Biting was inevitable. Probably it was too hurried. To safeguard radar stations from further attacks it was decreed that all of these sites should now be roundly protected by barbed wire. There had been a clear lack of adequate perimeter wiring at Bruneval, a deficiency which made as much of an impression on General Browning as it did on the Germans. Browning drew attention in his post-raid analysis to the need for all British radar sites and their attendant garrisons to be 'wired-in' and stressed that the wiring should be 'really good' in order to deter, or at least delay, a ground attack.[12] There was some obvious sense in this, of course, but as the RAF's hunt for more Würzburg installations continued, the Germans found to their cost they had failed to take into account the fact that barbed wire showed up particularly well on reconnaissance photographs taken from the air.

Demolishing the prominent villa at Bruneval was another questionable counter-measure adopted by the Germans after the 1942 raid. By that time the damage well and truly had been done.

In Britain the much trumpeted rip-roaring success of Operation Biting prompted an early expansion of the nation's airborne forces and had an immediate and profoundly positive effect on national morale. It was repeatedly featured for weeks afterwards in the British media, while an exuberant Churchill delighted in inviting Major Frost and some of his fellow officers to address a meeting of the War Cabinet on 5 March about the success of the daring mission,

Meanwhile, the raid had left a gaping wound in German radar strategy, without doubt a powerful strike in the wider radar war. It was bound to rankle, gnaw away at Nazi military pride and confidence in the continuing ability of the Third Reich to overcome the Allied foe, newly augmented by the USA's entry into the war following the Japanese attack on Pearl Harbor on 7 December 1941. What is rumoured to have happened off England's south coast in 1943 cannot be described as an exact parallel with Bruneval, but it does not seem unreasonable to conjecture on the possibility of a revenge raid by Germany on the Isle of Wight.

Chapter 5

Alfred Laurence: An Extraordinary Life

Rumours of a mid-war German raid on an Isle of Wight radar site, while common in the decades which immediately followed the conflict and always ardently told, could be characterised together as dramatically recounted stories handed down with very little in the way of authentic verification or reliable substance. Many islanders accepted that something of the sort must have happened and wondered why, as the years rolled by, official confirmation was still not forthcoming. For the same reason, a degree of scepticism took hold.

Thus the story acquired the status of a legend and this remained so until the 1980s when, from two quite separate sources, emerged powerful evidence to add the meat of authenticity to the dry, decaying bones of the island's story. The type of corroboration this provided was unique among the many tales of supposed enemy landings in Britain. The sources were German.

The first of these arrived courtesy of an Isle of Wight resident of German descent determined, in his own words, to 'blow the gaff' on what he was certain had been a significant historical event deliberately shrouded in a cloak of British secrecy ever since it had taken the nation's war leaders by surprise four decades earlier. His account was distinguished by the inclusion of substantial detail gilded by the stamp of authority from an apparently impeccable German source.

Dr Alfred Laurence had lived a truly extraordinary life prior to his arrival on the Isle of Wight. If we are to establish his credentials as standard-bearer for the veracity of the German raid legend, it is important to examine his life story, character and, if possible, the motivation for the remarkable zeal he demonstrated in his quest to finally turn the legend into accepted fact. And there is another, equally compelling, reason for such an examination. In its own right, the story of Alfred Laurence's life could probably sustain an absorbing book of some length.

He was born Alfred Lomnitz to Jewish parents in December 1910 at Breslau in what was then the Silesian lowlands of Germany and is now, renamed Wroclaw, the largest city in western Poland. An exceptionally gifted scholar, he was educated initially in his home town over a twelve-year period, attending the local gymnasium (the term for a German school preparing students for university) following his primary years' schooling. His subsequent move to France to study law at university was the springboard to an outstanding academic career which would ultimately see him awarded doctorates in chemistry and economics, as well as law, mastering an astonishing six languages along the way.

While in France, he used his burgeoning legal expertise to good effect, advising socialists and communists persecuted by the Nazi regime in his native country. Returning to Germany in 1936, he was, unsurprisingly, dispatched by the Hamburg Gestapo for 'political re-education' at Sachsenhausen concentration camp, which had opened that year in a suburb of Oranienburg, twenty-three miles north of Berlin's city centre. At school the young Lomnitz had been dismayed by the anti-Semitic views of some of his teachers. In Sachsenhausen his personal experience of German Jewish persecution at the hands of the SS was horrific.

Interviewed at length by German writer Hans Schmidt, he provided graphic accounts of his exposure to SS cruelties at the camp: Typically, on the slightest pretext, he and others were subjected to vile mistreatment by the guards using 'fists, kicks, sticks and weapons'. On one occasion Lomnitz was among a group of inmates who defiantly stood their ground when cajoled by an SS man to run away so that he could shoot them for trying to escape. There were some among the camp guards, he told Schmidt, 'whose most definite aim was to kill, nothing less than to kill, human beings for their own pleasure ... like a cat killing a captured mouse.'

In February 1937 Alfred Lomnitz was transferred into the hands of the Bavarian SS at Dachau, the first of the Nazi concentration camps when it was constructed in March 1933 on the site of a former gunpowder and munitions factory southeast of Dachau's medieval town which itself lay ten miles to the northwest of Munich. According to Schmidt, he arrived there with 'a scar from an SS helmet on his forehead.' Assigned to the 'Jew block', he was now under the direct control of *Oberscharführer* Vinzenz Schöttl, whose burgeoning notoriety as a callous anti-Semite thug – a reputation that would ultimately see him executed in 1946 as a war criminal – was clearly all too apparent at Dachau. Schmidt recorded prisoner Lomnitz's memorable description of Schöttl, as 'a giant with reddish hair, heavily built with enormous hands'.

Evidently, Vinzenz Schöttl's presence in the camp was equally and unpleasantly huge. Added Lomnitz:

'He spent a great amount of time in our block, gave orders regarding all details, checked and controlled minutely that we were conforming, and even exceeding, all required standards of cleanliness, orderliness and behaviour. Whoever was in the slightest way slack or otherwise "noticed" for any reason in his routine was in immediate danger.'

Schmidt wrote that 'working on a construction site in the camp was like being in the front line during the war; one could always be hit by a bullet, could never quite relax and never knew what was in store.' On one occasion, when Lomnitz could not push an overloaded wheelbarrow on the gravelly ground fast enough,

'he was ill-treated by the guard while Schoettl was watching. In the evening, as the block-leader inspected his ranks before roll-call, he remembered the incident and selected Lomnitz for a *Woatschn* – a slap with the hand on the ears. The victim realised the danger of being remembered permanently and finished off in time.'

While Lomnitz was spared the worst excesses of the Bavarian block-leader's ill-treatment, thanks in part to Schoettl learning of his love of music, an interest shared by both men, and a common dislike, judiciously implied on Lomnitz's part, of all things Prussian, it did not mean that Alfred was safe from the brutality meted out by other guards at Dachau camp. Added Hans Schmidt:

'Shortly before his release he had to stand at attention near the main entrance gate as an SS non-commissioned officer who happened to walk by noticed the yellow patch of the Jew on [his] uniform and delivered a savage blow with his fist into Lomnitz's face.'

During the eight months of his martyrdom in block six at Dachau, twenty-five of Lomnitz's fellow Jews died as a result of their miserable treatment by the guards. In his account which, in its general descriptive tone, is mirrored by the statements and memories of several other pre-war Nazi camp victims, Lomnitz noted that 'one or two [Jews] were openly murdered by the SS.'[1]

Lomnitz's discharge from Dachau on 1 October 1937 came after his family pleaded, via their lawyer, for sponsorship in the advertising columns of *The Times* in London. 'At that time,' wrote Hans Schmidt, 'the SS were willing to free prisoners in exchange for cash and proof of consequent emigration.' Geoffrey Wells, a writer unknown to the Lomnitz family, paid the ransom and offered a ticket of passage on a boat bound for England. After a few days with his parents in Breslau, Lomnitz travelled to the southern French port of Marseilles and embarked for London. Six months later, he left England for Bombay (Mumbai) in India, a home to Jewish settlers since the eighteenth century, attracted initially by economic opportunities. Here, he wrote detailed reflections of his experiences as a Jewish victim of Nazi hatred.[2]

Meanwhile, there was sad news from Germany for Lomnitz. His father had committed suicide when one of his housing tenants, an SS man, refused to pay rent, demanded the legal transfer of the house to himself and threatened Herr Lomnitz with the concentration camp if he did not comply. According to Hans Schmidt's collected essays, Alfred's distraught mother had taken the same poison as her husband but was saved by her maid and managed to join Alfred and his brother in Bombay. Events took a further tragic twist when, on the outbreak of world war in September 1939, the Lomnitz brothers were both arrested by the British authorities and consigned as German nationals to an internment camp. It proved too much for their mother; she took an overdose of sleeping pills and this time succeeded in taking her own life.

Alfred Lomnitz was finally able to escape this traumatic period of his life through emigration to the USA. In 1941 he found shelter in Philadelphia with an aunt and soon afterwards, reflecting his admiration for Lawrence of Arabia, a boyhood hero, changed his surname to Laurence, altering the spelling in order to make it easier to pronounce for the city's native French speakers. The American declaration of war following the December

1941 Japanese attack on Pearl Harbor presented the opportunity for the avowed anti-Nazi and now US citizen to play an active role in the defeat of National Socialism in the country of his birth and the wider stranglehold on democracy it exercised in collaboration with its Axis allies.

He applied for active military service in 1942 and, although accepted into the army, found himself initially detailed to hospital duty as a latrine orderly in a VD clinic for black recruits. This at least gave him a military foothold and, transferred to the infantry, he was sent to Europe in December 1943 as a technical sergeant in charge of fuel. Reaching Paris the following autumn as part of the Allied advance after D-Day, he was introduced to Colonel David Chavez Jnr, who had interrupted his civil career as a judge to serve for a second time in the army.

Chavez was amassing evidence of Nazi barbarity, specifically at Dachau, and had been alerted, apparently by Pope Pius XII himself, to rumours of the torturing of Roman Catholic clerics among the large concentration of religious leaders regarded as enemies of the Nazi state in the *Priesterblock* (priest barracks) at Dachau. The colonel immediately recognised the obvious worth of adding a former Dachau prisoner to his investigative team and obtained Laurence's transfer to the unit as a recorder. It was not long before he was effectively serving as Chavez's personal advisor, interpreter and guide. The team followed close behind the US front units and reached Dachau itself in the early morning of 30 April 1945, the day after the overcrowded concentration camp had been liberated by divisions of the US 7th Army.[3]

Admitted to the camp, Chavez and Laurence were on their way to visit the American commander who now had control of the place when they were stopped by a crowd of people. Laurence described hearing a 'horrible outcry' and seeing a man fall to the ground. 'An axe had totally split his skull,' he recalled. The victim was an SS guard who had hoped to escape by donning the uniform of a prisoner but had been recognised by some of the real inmates and killed on the spot, 'where his body remained all that day and the following day too'.

Laurence, 'stunned and confused' because the camp barely resembled the place he had left in 1937, was alerted to a group of SS guards seeking protection in a back room of the main building. 'Pistol in hand,' recorded

Schmidt, 'Laurence entered it with some American soldiers, arrested over ten SS men, led them out with raised arms and protected them from the rage of the prisoners.' With his own experiences at the hands of the SS in Dachau and Sachsenhausen still a relatively recent memory, it is probably safe to conclude that the emotions swirling in the mind of Alfred Laurence as he carried out this task were in absolute turmoil.

'The following two weeks were the most important in Laurence's life in respect of his personal contribution to the process of justice and fairness in the history of humanity,' added Schmidt. As he helped Chavez search for evidence to expose the full horror of Nazi perversion and persecution in Dachau camp so that its perpetrators could later be held to account, Laurence recoiled at the sight of US soldiers meting out a more immediate form of justice. 'Killings took place while we were present – captured SS men were killed,' he told Schmidt. Even the officer who had handed over the camp to the Americans had been shot by them. Laurence recalled entering rooms where SS guards were being interrogated by Intelligence officers of the combat troops in a way that Colonel Chavez would never have permitted:

'There was shouting, there were tears, even blood, and an emotional attitude, everybody excited, under nervous tension, unpleasant, totally unsmiling and thus un-American.'

Laurence found a great many lists of SS personnel and even his prisoner card of 1937. He translated the conversation of his superior with the soon to be infamous Professor Claus Schilling, the German tropical medicine specialist, whose wife invited American officers to her home in Dachau. When Schilling declared that not more than ten per cent of his camp inmate patients in the malaria experiment station had died, Chavez had him arrested on the spot.

During May 1945, Laurence compiled a list of forty-four incidents at Dachau that could definitely be classed as criminal specific incidents. These included the hanging of prisoners whose hands were chained behind their backs, the execution of ninety Russian officers in September 1944 and the poisoning of three patients in the 'malaria station' by an antipyretic (fever-reducing) drug. His work helped Chavez to send two powerful volumes of interviews and a slimmer introductory volume to his brother, Dennis, a member of the US Senate. In the same month Laurence was transferred to another team which worked in the vicinity of Salzburg. After his promotion to lieutenant, he investigated murders of American bomber crews in southern Germany before being ordered back to Dachau where he was detailed with Chavez to the prosecution team assembled for the first trial of the camp's indicted Nazi war criminals.

Much of Schmidt's detailed account of his interviews with Laurence focussed on the initial Dachau tribunal, which opened in November 1945 within the walls of the concentration camp itself and, unlike the international military trials of leading Nazi figures in Nuremberg, was conducted exclusively by personnel representing the US Army as the liberating Allied force. From this we are able to discern a good deal about Laurence's approach to the legal process and his specific role within it, and thereby gain valuable insight into the character, conduct and motivation of the man who would later champion the cause of revealing what he was sure was the truth behind the closely-guarded secret of a mid-war German landing on the Isle of Wight.

'I had to fulfil a duty, come with a mission which dated way back to 1937 or before, and while I did not want to be found overzealous and too keen to see this trial carried through, I was ... totally in agreement with the main purpose of the show for which we were setting the stage and which I could help to see performed,' said Laurence in recalling his pre-trial emotions. At times during the trial, he told Schmidt, he could hardly keep his eyes dry. This is not difficult to understand, of course, but Laurence's thoughts were conflicting. 'He might at the same time feel for an accused SS man yet also remember what the SS as a whole had stood for,' added Schmidt in the process of establishing a core element of the Laurence psyche.

Laurence had slammed the moral judgment of those among the American prosecutors who came 'with a vengeance ... totally biased from the very start'. These men, wrote Schmidt, 'did not adhere to the principles of fairness and impartiality which Laurence lived up to adamantly'. Reinforcing this view, Schmidt recorded how Laurence, who proved a diligent and effective prosecutor at the trial, was nonetheless deeply reluctant to rely on the ready enthusiasm of some 'highly emotional and mentally exhausted' Dachau survivors to testify, as he put it, 'against whoever we might name'. In the context of judicial fairness, his moral code was disturbed by the 'seduction' of witnesses who, as Schmidt noted, 'were well quartered and had access to coveted American goods such as cigarettes, soap and razor blades.'

Laurence's refusal to be clouded by single-minded determination to win at all costs evidently extended to his admiration for the defence attorneys. According to Schmidt, he respected the defence team, was full of praise for them and called them 'excellent trial lawyers'. Laurence made clear his overriding consideration at the trial was that it should be seen as 'a warning for the future'. This was the basic aim, 'not just to get some forty poor devils convicted according to the book, perhaps strung up because they happened to be the ones we could get hold of.' The lesson, he stressed, 'had to be drawn, the facts clearly stated, the causes explored, the criminals brought before their judges.' But it had to be done properly, with justice to the fore, if a repeat of the inhumanity personified in Hitler was to be avoided.

Laurence felt the trial succeeded in fulfilling this aim – the victory had been won. The evidence was well presented, evidence 'the excellent defence could not undo in spite of their great efforts and occasional brilliance.' He added:

'In no single case could the chain be broken [and] the final results – thirty-six condemnations to death, four to much minor sentences, yet not a single acquittal – were the correct ones, not only premeditated by us in line with the desired political effect but genuinely derived from the cases presented and arrived at by just judges.'[4]

Of the thirty-six sentenced to death, twenty-eight were executed, including Professor Schilling, and eight had their sentences commuted to prison terms, which none had to serve in full. As for Laurence, from what he told Hans Schmidt, he emerges as a man with the deepest of convictions for the twin causes of truth and justice, a man of the utmost integrity. While he would be terribly scarred by his exposure to the cruellest extremes of Nazi ideology, something that would haunt him and those closest to him for years to come, his compassion and extraordinary regard for humanity is surely the beacon we should carry into any assessment of his credentials as a reliable source of information in the quest to expose the truth behind the legendary German wartime landing on the Isle of Wight. But first we should examine the remainder of his life story, paying particular regard to another extraordinary chapter in the story.

Following the war Laurence worked as a technologist for 3M, the US industrial conglomerate which had set its post-war sights on overseas expansion. 'My father was sent over to the UK to oversee the research and development branch in London,' recalled his son, Geoffrey. By 1952–53 the family – Alfred, his wife Ilse (Lotte), the couple's elder son, Thomas (born in June 1945 to Lottie and her first husband, whose marriage ended the same year, and adopted by Alfred) and Geoffrey, born in December 1949 – had moved to London. In May 1956, the family's size had grown with the birth of a daughter, Virginia. Dr Laurence remained with 3M until around 1961, having returned several times to the US while in the company's employment. 'I don't know why he left 3M,' added Geoffrey, 'but in 1962 we moved to Nassau in the Bahamas, where he worked for IDI, an investment and development group.'

A year later, thanks to another change in Alfred's employment, the family were back in England and were now living in the Surrey town of Purley, although Dr Laurence's new post with the United Nations Educational, Scientific and Cultural Organisation (UNESCO) was actually based in Paris. Geoffrey remembered his father making several trips to the Middle East, specifically the Persian (now Iranian) capital of Tehran, during this period and recalled that he was involved in the extraordinary 1967 Abu Simbel project near the Egyptian border with Sudan – the relocation of massive rock temples dating back to the thirteenth century BC to prevent their being submerged during creation of the huge artificial water reservoir of Lake Nasser.

Drama had stalked the life of Dr Laurence – and this was set to continue. 'He worked at UNESCO until the 1969 fiasco,' added his son. The fiasco in question was remarkable in the extreme. By the spring of that year Alfred had become a controversial topic for debate in Parliament after his Surrey house was surrounded by Special Branch police officers and a detachment of men from MI5 – reportedly, though this was later challenged in Parliament, a total interrogative force of fifty! The police were armed with a warrant issued under the Official Secrets Act. Laurence, just back from holiday, had no choice other than to allow the wholly unexpected and unwelcome visitors to raid his home and search him in his living room.

'They asked me to sit down in this chair and empty my pockets, and then immediately to take off all my clothes,' he told ITN *News at Ten's* Gerald Seymour in an interview, his first on the incident, broadcast three weeks later on 7 May. 'I thought at first they were going to look at my jacket, but then I had to take off my tie, then my shirt and my shoes – they looked very carefully at the heels of my shoes and into the buckle of my belt, and, well, I was completely bare.'

Had he protested? Laurence was asked. 'No, I'll tell you, I've been a prisoner in Nazi concentration camps … this immediately came to my mind; the memories of thirty years ago.' Did he have any complaints about the way he was treated? 'No … well you see I didn't even think of complaining. I had no idea who these gentlemen were and my mind doesn't work like that. I had an idea there was something very important going on and somebody had committed a very grave error as far as I was concerned – I had been taken for somebody else.'

Laurence was taken to nearby Kenley police station for what he described as 'pretty tough' further questioning. 'I have done a lot of interrogating myself,' he told Seymour. 'I was a wartime investigator and I interrogated prisoners of war, so I know something about it, but it was a pretty stiff performance.' It had been sophisticated – definitely a good interrogation, he said, adding that the questioning had extended from mid-afternoon until about one in the morning, 'practically without interruption.' His inquisitors were 'very intelligent people, with excellent training, but of course they were not friendly. They were trying to find out things which I had done against the law, and they were trying, whatever I said, to trip me or make me feel that they understood much better – that I was hiding things or that I was … covering up.'

There had, he said, been no shouting; no raised voices at all, 'but you see, the point was that I was confronted with a dossier. I realised very soon … that they were asking [questions] from a book. One man, 'obviously the head of the interrogation' according to Laurence, followed the book closely; others recorded his answers in writing, 'occasionally interfering with questions of their own.' It was one of these men who tried to 'throw' him with repeated suggestions that he was not telling the truth. 'He tried to pull me off my story,' Laurence added.

Cold War tensions lay at the heart of this dramatic 1969 encounter. Alfred Laurence was suspected of being a Russian agent – at the least, a man with communist leanings and direct links to the Soviet intelligence service. The British agencies, it transpired, believed they had good reason to suspect him. 'What did they accuse you of? Anything?' asked Gerald Seymour.

Dr Laurence's reply was both candid and fulsome – and, on the face of it, startling. He clearly had no intention of keeping the details to himself. 'At the beginning they went through my personal life story ... in so much detail that, well, it took two hours or more. Then they came out with what they were actually after. "You have been in contact with Russian intelligence," they said, and then of course I realised, all of a sudden, what the whole thing was about. I told them, "yes" and this in turn floored them; they weren't prepared for that ... thinking that I was probably going to be somebody who was in contact [with the Soviet Union] and would deny it.'

His interrogators were, he thought, 'possibly quite relieved' as well as surprised at his ready admission. 'Then I said I had been in contact with Russian intelligence in Berlin [at the end of the war],' something he felt sure would have been in the dossier. 'But when I said I had also been in contact in this country [the UK] they literally gasped – they hadn't expected that.'

To camera, Seymour revealed that Dr Laurence had once done 'minor work' for American intelligence, the CIA, the implication being that he might well have been of interest to the Russians. Laurence, however, was adamant that he had not sought contact with the Soviets and was certainly not seeking to work for them. The ITN man told viewers that his interviewee had first been approached by a Russian agent in 1965, the contact made via a telephone call to his home. Other conversations had followed, apparently face to face. 'If, as you say, you had no intention of engaging in espionage in this country, why did you go through these meetings in this country with members of Russian intelligence?' Seymour asked.

'Well,' replied Laurence, 'the police asked me the same question. The first time [of contact] I didn't even think about it. The second time I began to be curious about what they really wanted.' It was linked to a trade mission he was told by the Russian who spoke to him. When contact was made for a third time he had felt decidedly uneasy. 'I felt I must stop this because I had begun to get very, very worried about the whole story. Being an alien living in England I didn't want to have any contacts I didn't like. Frankly, I was seriously worried ... by that time.'

'Why didn't you go ... to any of the authorities [in Britain] if you were worried, as you say you were, about the contacts?' Gerald Seymour asked him – on the face of it, an obvious question.

'Going to the British authorities as an alien was not in my line of duty,' replied Laurence. 'My idea was to go and tell the men I had known in the CIA, which I actually did in 1967. They had definitely been to see me as an American, though there was nothing I could really tell them except that people had called me and tried to give me money. What would it have been if I had gone to the British authorities and told them the story? They would have only said, "well, here's a foreigner, he has contacted the Russians, he is undesirable – out with him!"' And that, he added, he was very anxious to avoid, pointing out that he had two British-born children, Thomas and Virginia, who were both pursuing their education in the UK.

Asked by Seymour what were his feelings about espionage, Dr Laurence concluded the interview with an unequivocal statement of distaste. 'In wartime, espionage is probably necessary to shorten war, but in peacetime I think it's horrific. It is something I personally and certainly wouldn't want to have the slightest connection with – I consider it one of the most deplorable affairs that are going on right now. The spy mania makes me absolutely sick.'

It was a particularly good scoop for ITN and later in the month, with the story now attracting worldwide media interest and speculation, the strange case of Alfred Laurence's brush with British intelligence became a subject for Parliamentary debate. On 21 May the matter was raised in the House of Lords by the Bishop of Southwark, Mervyn Stockwood, a man noted for his often controversially radical Anglican views.[5] Was the government, he asked, 'satisfied that the actions of Dr Alfred Laurence, ... have in any way offended against the Official Secrets Act of 1911?' Vociferously, the bishop, in whose diocese Laurence lived, criticised Harold Wilson's Labour government for its failure to issue a clarifying statement on the matter, pointing to 'considerable public concern' and the detrimental effect the continuing lack of a formal governmental response was having on Laurence's livelihood and status.

With support from elsewhere in the chamber, Stockwood's intervention had the desired effect. A day later the requested statement from Home Secretary James Callaghan was relayed to the Lords. It read:

> 'In April, information was received from a KGB agent who had defected to the West that Dr Laurence had been recruited in 1963 to work for the KGB. A number of interviews have taken place with Dr Laurence and the assessment of the case is now complete ... the Attorney General has come to the conclusion that, on the available information, there are no grounds for taking proceedings against Dr Laurence under the Official Secrets Act.'

The peers had their answer and, while there would be further debate in the House about the 'unfair' treatment of Laurence by the authorities, this extraordinary episode had reached its end.[6] It has since been given very little attention, but remains a vivid memory for his younger son.

'I was at St Martin's School of Art [in London] at the time, getting my BA,' recalled Geoffrey Laurence from his Santa Fe base in New Mexico, USA. Today a prominent realist painter whose works have been widely exhibited across the US and in Europe, he remembered driving to Purley in May 1969 so he could meet his parents on their return from holiday.

> 'There was a big brown van in the driveway,. I let myself in to be greeted by a house-full of MI5 and policemen. I was not to leave again for a week, under constant supervision. I could not even go to the toilet without a policeman present, I suppose in case I flushed away an important piece of hidden evidence! We were all kept separate in the house, always under close supervision. They were tearing up every single thing in the place, including the food in the fridge! What they were looking for they obviously did not find. [My father was] kept naked in the dining room while they were questioning him – I saw it for a brief moment when I opened the door by surprise – and then they took him off [Geoffrey thought it was to Bow Street police station

in Covent Garden] for a couple of weeks. As he had been through the rise of the Nazis and incarceration in Sachsenhuasen and Dachau, I guess that was nothing new to him, though this time from the British Government instead. He sued for an official apology afterwards but was unsuccessful. Nicolas Tomalin [an English journalist and writer who worked for several national newspapers and whose father was Miles Tomalin, the communist poet and veteran of the Spanish Civil War] was going to write an article or book with him to try and clear his name, but I don't know if anything was ever published.'

Nicolas Tomalin died in October 1973. There is no obvious record of him publishing anything about Laurence and that opens the door to conjecture. What should we make of all this?

If, despite the apparently official British view to the contrary, Laurence *was* a Soviet agent, he must have been a very good one indeed, capable of outwitting the UK's security service when the net closed around him. If, on the other hand, he was nothing of the sort, as seems far more likely the case, did he emerge from this shockingly degrading experience with a grudge against the UK authorities? Despite choosing to remain in Britain, did this fester in his mind until he grasped an opportunity, years later, to embarrass his adopted country by reinforcing the legend that its long-cherished boast of invincibility against any kind of landing on its shores by German armed forces during World War Two was, in fact, a fallacy? He would be able to point to very persuasive evidence of the raid's authenticity and so could argue, justifiably, that he was merely serving the cause of historical integrity.

Or was the whole MI5 episode the proverbial storm in a teacup, whipped up by the turbulent events and consequences of Dr Laurence's remarkable life – and nothing to do with his later campaign to underscore the Isle of Wight's German raid legend with a rigid platform of solid fact? Was this much more to do with a continued fervent desire to uncover an unpalatable truth?

Chapter 6

Dietrich Andernacht: The Story from Germany

B y the time of his encounter with MI5 in 1969, Alfred Laurence had already established a close association with the Isle of Wight, specifically with the southern coastal village of St Lawrence. Appropriately, given the village's status as the preferred location for the rumoured German raid, it was from here that he elevated the story onto a whole new footing with the first detailed account of the legendary landing. With remarkable zeal, he set out to proclaim it loudly as a wholly factual incident which had been hushed up for decades by successive governments in the UK.

Earlier in the 1960s, Dr Laurence had purchased Craigie Lodge, a substantial property in Undercliff Drive, St Lawrence, as a holiday home. 'We spent several summers there,' Geoffrey Laurence recalled. In 1970, a year after the extraordinary brush with MI5, Alfred sold the house and bought another close by in the Channel-fringed village, La Mer in Seven Sisters Road, this time as a permanent residence. 'I rebuilt, enlarged and interior-decorated it over a two-year period in 1973–74,' his son remembered. 'My parents moved into the house in 1975 when he retired on a German compensation pension for his concentration camp years.'

The couple embraced life in St Lawrence. Taking a keen interest in local affairs and the area's heritage, both were stalwart members of the Undercliff Society and, following its formation in 1980, Ventnor & District Local History Society, which included St Lawrence within its breadth of local interest. In 1988, Dr Laurence underlined his obvious passion for the village in the form of a privately published book, *In Praise of St Lawrence: A Song at Twilight*, tracing the parish's ecclesiastical and social history.

But, undoubtedly, those years in the hands of Nazi tyranny had profoundly shaped his life and, according to his son, this was still very much an overriding factor at the time of his move with Lottie to the Isle of Wight and, indeed, in the years that followed at his island home.

'He was highly intelligent, brilliant, but he was also overburdened with the past thanks to his experiences of the war and his loss at that time [to Nazi persecution] of his parents and sister, not to mention the rest of his entire extended family His outward behaviour was very different to his behaviour behind the closed doors of family life, almost to the point of schizophrenia. I will say no more on that other than that it took until 1967 for me to get Mother to confirm to me that I was indeed Jewish. My relationship with him was not the happiest.'

To have hidden from his son such a crucial element of his upbringing is startling but, according to Geoffrey, it was in keeping with the secretive nature of Alfred (and also his wife) 'about a lot of things, including his working life and travels … when he died my mother, I suspect in a fit of vengefulness, burnt all his papers. He had eight filing cabinets full.'

In the words of Oskar Winter, a fellow former Dachau inmate, recorded in a 1990 interview for the British Library, Dr Laurence had 'left the Jewish faith and does not want to know about it anymore.' He was clearly the most complex of men, haunted and bedevilled by his past.[1]

Geoffrey Laurence pointed out:

'I had little contact with my father after they moved to the Isle of Wight, other than the usual public holidays etc. We did not get on and, as I have said, he was an extremely secretive man in certain areas. I still have no real idea if he was a spy, a double agent perhaps who worked for the CIA and/or the Russians, or neither of them. I will never know. Nearly all of his relatives were either gassed or worked to death, as were my mother's family, so I had been brought up in an atmosphere of underlying and unstated fear. I only saw my mother's parents once – my father's, of course, were dead before the war's end.'

It may be regarded as somewhat ironic that a man with such a secretive side should embrace the cause of exposing what he was convinced had been a national secret in Britain for many years.

I knew very little of his extraordinary background when, following publication in 1989 of the book I had written on the Isle of Wight's eventful war years, a mutual acquaintance alerted me to Dr Laurence's seemingly revelatory account of the mysterious German raid on an Isle of Wight radar station. I was given a copy of a letter he (Laurence) had written in April 1980 to Hilary Scammell, then the island's county reference librarian. Evidently, Dr Laurence had approached Miss Scammell months earlier with his assertion that there had been a German raid and had asked if the library service was aware of any local records which might confirm this.

His letter in 1980 was in response to one Miss Scammell had sent to him the previous October, with which she had enclosed a copied reply from the British Embassy in Bonn, the West German capital prior to re-unification of the German state, commenting on Dr Laurence's claims. It was apparent from Laurence's letter that the embassy had effectively rubbished the story. Stung by this, Dr Laurence had evidently retreated to the source of his tale.

It was clear that this had not proved a waste of his time. He told Miss Scammell:

'The attachment to your letter helped me to sway my German informant, Dr Dietrich Andernacht, the head of the City of Frankfurt (Main) archives, who had previously hesitated to help us with the requested historical information. When I talked to him two weeks ago, he finally agreed to follow up on this matter by investigating the German military records concerning the raid, in which he had personally participated. He promised to let me have his results in due course.'

So, according to Dr Laurence, not only was the source of his information a highly reputable German official, someone dedicated to the preservation and presentation of historical records, he had actually been a member of the wartime enemy force which had landed on the Isle of Wight!

The son of a teacher, Dietrich Andernacht was born in December 1921 at Keilhau, a village in the central German state of Thuringia. A gifted scholar, he attended the grammar school in Eisenach before pursuing an academic interest in history at the universities of Freiburg and Frankfurt am Main, his studies interrupted by the outbreak of war and service with the German military. Records indicate that in 1940, while advancing with his infantry unit during the Germans' all-conquering *Blitzkrieg* offensive in western Europe, he was seriously wounded and transferred to hospital for an extended period of treatment and recuperation. Returning to army service, he was eventually captured by the Americans in the latter stages of the war but survived the conflict without further mishap and was thus able to resume his university education back in Germany. This led to the award of a doctorate at Frankfurt in 1950 after completion of a biographical work on the life of Bishop (later Saint) Otto of Bamberg.[2]

Between 1952 and 1954 Andernacht trained at Marburg, Hessen, for what would prove a long and illustrious career as a civic archivist. Joining the archival service back in Frankfurt on completion of his training, his outstanding work there led to his appointment in 1959, just five years after his arrival, as chief city archivist, a position he would hold until his retirement in May 1984. Under his direction, the restructuring and management of Frankfurt's historically important archival collection was very successfully undertaken despite, according to the compilers of the city's biographical lexicon,[3] 'a constant battle against the indifference and ignorance of the municipal authorities'. Perhaps his greatest directorial achievement was to oversee the absorption in 1972 of a large percentage of the Frankfurt archives – records and artefacts dating back to the early Middle Ages – within new three-storey accommodation beneath the city's former Carmelite monastery; Andernacht was a man with a passion for the past.[4]

His friendship with Alfred Laurence almost certainly arose from Andernacht's deep interest in German Jewish history, primarily centred on the specific Jewish experience in Frankfurt. He kept in close contact with emigrants from Jewish families and representatives of the former Jewish community, and in 1961 founded a commission for an official study of the Jewish presence which included research projects, publications and exhibitions; this led to the establishment of Frankfurt's comprehensive Jewish Museum in 1988.

Renowned beyond the confines of Frankfurt am Main for his research into the legal, economic and social history of the city, the longstanding Jewish element of the city's overall story featured prominently among his accomplished published works. When failing health forced his premature 1984 retirement from the archival service, Dr Andernacht devoted his efforts to completion of what was undoubtedly his principal written work, a hugely acclaimed account of the history of Frankfurt's Jews in the medieval period and succeeding centuries, widely considered the most comprehensive review of a Jewish community in the late Middle Ages and early modern period. Together with co-author Eleanor Stirling he also published a well-received volume on the turbulent experience of the city's Jewish people between 1933 and 1945.[5]

For more than two decades, between 1960 and 1983, he managed the Frankfurt Historical Commission. His entry in the city's biographical lexicon continues:

> 'He worked as a prudent scientific organiser who encouraged research and editorial support of numerous publications. His personal modesty made him withdraw entirely behind the scientific tasks. He was a strict and critical scientist, methodologically correct and incorruptible, who remained averse to all fashionable and contemporary trends and political impositions. Instead, he promoted the unprejudiced [immersion] into sources and the sober process of historical knowledge.'

Here was a man whose integrity and dedication to the preservation and promulgation of historical knowledge surely could not be doubted. Indeed, to suggest otherwise, to doubt his word on a historical incident in which he was himself involved, would amount to an insult. There was no plausible reason for him to fabricate the story of a German wartime raid on the Isle of Wight, embroider it or in any other way provide details designed to mislead, and clearly there was absolutely nothing in his known character or status to suggest that he would do this or even contemplate it. Anything he had told Alfred Laurence about the legendary raid, assuming Laurence had correctly interpreted it, had to be treated with the utmost respect.

And it appeared from Dr Laurence's 1980 letter to Isle of Wight librarian Hilary Scammell that by that time Dietrich Andernacht had already told him a very great deal. It was riveting stuff!

'From his verbal advice,' Laurence wrote, 'I now see thy whole operation as much more complex than I had previously surmised.' Within the following lines of typescript the details flowed:

'The raiding party from Alderney did not only land on the Wight, obtain their objective – a broadcasting or emission device of considerable size, made of metal, which they returned to their experts, who managed to make it function properly at their own base – and return in their vessel to base. They also took several British prisoners with them, probably three men, and there was a skirmish. The equipment had an automatic self-destructive device, and this did indeed function when the Germans dismantled [it], blowing two large holes into the "box."

'But the base contents remained undamaged so that the Germans could indeed elicit the technical secret from this object, which had been the specific target of their well-prepared raid. Their prisoners obviously were the guards who they surprised in the hut where the emitter was housed. They resisted and Dr Andernacht explained that they [the raiders] were surprised with their success – also that they managed to bring their booty back to working order.

'He was not the CO of the mission, which was organised by a *Genesende-Kompanie* consisting of men who had been wounded elsewhere and were sent to Alderney to complete their recovery while being used for minor military duties – such as the Isle of Wight raiding party.'

On the face of it, this description of the party's composition is entirely plausible. The *Genesende-Kompanie* (convalescent company) was a component of the complex *Ersatzhee* (German Replacement Army) system which operated throughout the war. Military historian W. Victor Madej, a prolific writer on the organisation of the Wehrmact's order of battle, has neatly summarised the wide-ranging role of the replacement army, set up in each of the military districts within Germany. It oversaw the

'conscription, training and replacement of personnel, including control of mobilisation policies and the actual call-up of men; all types of military training, including the selection and schooling of officers and non-commissioned officers; the dispatch of personnel replacements to field units … and the organisation of new units.'[6]

According to Victor Madej, the normal location of a replacement unit under this ingenious reservist system was the home station of its affiliated operational field unit, to which soldiers would expect ultimately to return for their discharge or for reassignment.

> 'For example, a [field unit] soldier who was wounded and went to a reserve hospital in the "zone of the interior" (i.e. Germany) would be sent, upon leaving the hospital, to his affiliated *Ersatz* unit before being returned to the field.'

It was, however, not always as straightforward a transition as this. Previously wounded or sick men might instead find themselves attached temporarily to a *Genesende-Kompanie* and assigned the type of light duties considered appropriate to usefully complete their recuperation and fine-tune their preparedness for eventual return to the field unit. A commando-style raid from occupied territory on a relatively accessible coastal English target, potentially offering both strategic and symbolic reward, would seem to fit that bill. Given the established fact that Dietrich Andernacht is known to have been wounded during his army service in the earlier part of the war, he clearly fits the profile for the raiding party.

The clear reference in the Laurence/Andernacht story to the taking of British prisoners is a particularly interesting detail in that it is reflected in perhaps the most repeated local version of the 'raid on the radar' legend. This is a compelling tale laced with a large dose of mystery, intrigue and frustrating incompleteness. It was featured, for example, in prolific Isle of Wight writer Jan Toms' charming miscellany of historical tit-bits, *The Little Book of the Isle of Wight*, published in 2011 by The History Press in Stroud, although she places her story a year earlier than the more usually quoted 1943:

> 'Contrary to claims that no German military set foot in Britain during the Second World War, a secret raid was allegedly carried out at St Lawrence in 1942. The target was the radar installation and, in a lightning attack, German soldiers scaled the cliffs then departed again for the Channel Islands. What they achieved is uncertain but to avoid

panic the incident was hushed up. It may never have come to light had not at least one British soldier vanished. Officially, he was thought to have fallen from the cliff and drowned, his body washed away. Imagine the joy when his family apparently received a post-card from a PoW camp announcing that he was alive.'

Hinting strongly, to say the very least, at a wartime British cover-up, the tale has been augmented down the years in several ways. One account places at the heart of it a local Ventnor girl who had been going out with one of the troops stationed at St Lawrence radar site on guard duty. One day she went to meet him and was told to her dismay that he had died. Again, the explanation was that he had fallen down the cliff and sustained fatal injuries. Then, months later, she received news that he was, in fact, alive and well in a German PoW camp.

The story closely mirrors a further account featured in an *Island Life* magazine article from 2009 by June Efford recalling various aspects of the Isle of Wight's multi-faceted war.[7] The writer recounted a tale handed down to islander Kevin Dakin by his late mother, 'a story of when she was a Wren on the island in 1944. It appears that when a young soldier guarding a searchlight unit disappeared it was supposed that he had fallen off a cliff. But some time later a Red Cross post-card came through saying he had been snatched by a German raiding party and was a prisoner of war.' This account is possibly unique, both in suggesting the raid was mounted in 1944 which, given the war situation at the time, seems highly improbable, and in its specific reference to a searchlight unit, a point of detail which cannot summarily be ruled out.

Yet another version tells of a British soldier imprisoned by the enemy who was told by a fellow inmate that he had been 'captured on the Isle of Wight by Germans'. Puzzled, his post-war attempts to substantiate the baffling story met with a series of blank responses – nobody could, or was willing to, suggest how such an unlikely outcome could possibly have been true.

Quite apart from how the presumed lack of funerals and inquests were explained to family and friends of those British soldiers who, according to officialdom, had sustained fatal injuries in a cliff fall, what all of these stories lack are names, crucially those of the men who had been taken prisoner, whether this was one, two or, as Dr Laurence had suggested, as many as three men. There are certainly no records with which to verify these persistent accounts. The usual, and tempting, conclusion is that, if British servicemen really were taken captive by a German raiding party in the course of an assault on an Isle of Wight radar station, on their release from wartime captivity, or very soon afterwards, they would surely have been told to sign the Official Secrets Act or otherwise dissuaded from saying anything about this to anybody back home.[8]

Having already provided by far the most comprehensive account of the story, Dr Laurence concluded his letter to Miss Scammell by promising to write again 'once Dr Andernacht provides me with the promised additional information'. On learning of this intriguing correspondence a decade or so later I sought a meeting with him at his home. Given the length of time that had elapsed, there seemed every chance that he would have gleaned significant further detail from his German contact. Anticipation, however, was tempered by the fact that nothing had emerged publically since the exchange of letters in 1979–80 to 'blow the gaff' – as Alfred Laurence had promised – on the story of the raid. What did this mean? Had Dr Laurence lost interest? Had Dr Andernacht back-tracked and decided against going public? Was it possible that officialdom in Britain had intervened – had Dr Laurence been got at?

There was certainly no indication of the first and third of those possibilities when I met with Alfred Laurence at his delightful home overlooking the English Channel. As we chatted in his well-stocked library he seemed pleased at my interest in his take on the story. Full of charm and good humour, he reiterated the contents of his correspondence with the island's library service and struck me as a man of deep intelligence and integrity, not someone prone to inventing sensational tales of wartime derring-do. It has recently been suggested to me that during his years of Isle of Wight residency Fred Laurence (as he was generally known locally) tended at times to develop 'a bee in his bonnet' when pursuing something of importance to him. However, while he was clearly animated by his story from Germany and the need for it to be publically acknowledged, the overriding impression he gave when I spoke with him in 1992 was that of a keen student of history anxious to put the record straight.

He explained that he and Dietrich Andernacht had been friends for a considerable time and it was clear he held the now retired 70-year-old archivist and eminent historian in the highest regard. Fred Laurence was certain that what his friend had told him of the Isle of Wight raid was true. It *had* taken place and it was about time the world knew about it. However, it seemed Dr Andernacht had not divulged anything further about the incident since the two men had discussed it back in 1980. He was, explained Dr Laurence, 'nervous about the furore he feels it will cause in both Britain and Germany. I don't think he feels able to cope with that now.'

While understandable, this obviously came as a disappointment, but Fred Laurence's next words were more encouraging – if somewhat qualified by an intriguing new piece of information:

'He might tell you something if you were to contact him directly and mention my name but, as I understand it, he is not keen on saying much about it now. Instead, he has written a full account of the raid and instructed his lawyers to hold on to this until after his death.'

If a man of Dr Andernacht's reputation and undisputed integrity had taken the trouble to compile a detailed account of a wartime incident with which he was personally involved, there had to be something in this. So long as he was able to confirm what Fred Laurence had claimed, the story would acquire a unique historical quality, distinguished from all other tales of Second World War enemy landings in the UK by highly reputable evidence from Germany.

How much, if anything, would Dietrich Anderbacht be willing to tell me? Provided by Fred Laurence with his home address in Frankfurt, I wrote to him in October 1992, enclosing a copy of my book on the Isle of Wight's war years and seeking his help in establishing the truth, or otherwise, behind the major story I had been unable to incorporate because of what I had imagined at the time was a complete lack of credible evidence to support it. Having pointed out in the letter that there appeared to be no accessible British archival records, I set out the facts according to Dr Laurence so that, even if he felt unable to elaborate on the story at this stage, it would be simple for Dr Andernacht to either confirm or deny the Laurence account.

He might also be able to throw some light over one puzzling aspect of that account. Although Fred Laurence, in his letter to Hilary Scammell, had not referred to a specific locational target for the raid, it was clear when I spoke with him that he had assumed it had been RAF Ventnor's radar station on the summit of St Boniface Down, although he was open to the view that the far more easily accessible RAF St Lawrence, the former site of which lay only a short walk from his home in the village, might well have been the more probable option. The facts he had gleaned from Dietrich Andernacht had lacked any reference to the onward progress of the raiding party to their targeted site once they had come ashore on the Isle of Wight.

When it arrived, the eagerly-awaited reply from Dr Andernacht was as concise as it was utterly charming – fifteen lines of typed German text on a blank post-card. He began by thanking me for the book. 'Your remarkable gift came as a surprise to me,' read the English translation. 'Many thanks. It seems fitting that a dear old acquaintance, Dr Alfred Laurence, has given me in this way a stimulating experience. I am convinced of the thoroughness of your work. My endorsement will not disappoint you then.' This was kind of him, of course, but more importantly it provided immediate confirmation, should I have doubted it, of his evidently close links with Fred Laurence, key purveyor in the UK of the German landing story.

But what of the legendary incident itself? There was no elaboration – it was more a matter of what Dr Andernacht did *not* say. He did not deny or seek to amend any of the repeated facts I had put to him. It was tempting, therefore, to conclude that, essentially, Fred Laurence had provided an account with which Dietrich Andernacht concurred. His next sentence was the most significant of his short response:

'Memories of events are worth little when official records which would substantiate them beyond doubt are not to hand. If there are no British records, then German ones. A considerable raid of this size *must* be recorded in the official records.'

Having made this intriguing point, he apologised for his 'formless post-card' and explained that, 'to all intents and purposes, since the beginning of the year I have given up writing letters.'

In terms of its length, or lack of it, and the absence of any new detail, Dr Andernacht's reply did not amount to much. In terms of its core message, however, this appeared to be a very significant step forward in the quest to reach the truth. Not only had he not attempted to gainsay Fred Laurence's story, his words suggested an inside knowledge and recall of the incident – with a strong hint that its scale may have been markedly more than that of a minor operation – and his belief that somewhere either side of the wartime divide records would exist.

It had always seemed possible, if not probable, that Germany would have compiled and then archived documentation to corroborate an apparently successful landing on UK soil. But where was it? Had it survived the catastrophic collapse of the Nazi regime in 1945? In responding to Dr Andernacht I stressed that I had not seen, or been aware of, any official documentary evidence in either country to confirm the story. Therefore, his memories of the commando raid would prove invaluable. I did not want to push it any further. My hope was that, even if he did feel unable to provide anything in the way of a first-hand account, he might at least be prepared to point me in the direction of any relevant official German records.

I had one specific request. I asked if he had recorded the exact date of the raid, pointing out that this obviously would assist any search for archival records in both Germany and the UK.

In January 1993, Dr Andernacht replied. The tone was again friendly but his message was succinct – this time confined to just six lines of typescript on an otherwise blank post-card. He addressed just the specific point about the timing of the raid. 'The date you are seeking for should be found in May 1943. I must admit, however, that I am not entirely sure of this,' he wrote.

Despite this uncertainty, the very fact that he had suggested an approximate date was hugely encouraging, not only in narrowing significantly the probable period for further research – until then there had been virtually no indication of a date for the raid – but also because it underlined impressively the likelihood that the legendary Isle of Wight landing had been a fact.

It was, therefore, a pity, one I bitterly regret, that circumstances and other commitments prevented me from pursuing the story further other than to issue periodic appeals for information via the news media and internet, and to several selected audiences. The years passed, no collaborative material had surfaced from national archival sources and by the time I was able to resume research on the 'raid on the radar' legend for this book the intervening years had seen the passing of both Alfred Laurence and Dietrich Andernacht. With health failing, Laurence and his wife had left the Isle of Wight to spend the final period of their lives close to their daughter in Swanage, Dorset. Alfred had reached the age of 96 before his death in 2007. Dr Amdernacht had died in November 1996, a few weeks short of his 75th birthday. As for Andernacht's supposedly written account of the raid, this has never emerged despite the efforts of city archival staff in Frankfurt to find it. Possibly that bit of the story really was a myth.[9]

I asked Geoffrey Laurence in 2016 if his father had ever mentioned Dr Andernacht. In reply, Geoffrey told me:

'I have no knowledge of him, nor of most of my father's friends and acquaintances. I did meet some but have forgotten their names and who they were. He did have a friend called Barney who taught at Charterhouse School [Surrey]. He had apparently been in Dachau as well as my father, always attended the camp reunions and was on the Dachau committee along with my father. My mother would scowl at Barney behind my father's back and whispered to me once, "do you know how long he was in the camp ... only three weeks!" Perhaps Dietrich Andernacht was also connected in some way with the concentration camps?'

From what is known of Dr Andernacht's war service, and indeed his wider life, this seems improbable. As noted, a shared interest in the history of German Jewish experience is more likely. Whatever the precise nature of their relationship, the joint testimony from the two men has to be regarded as powerful evidence from the German perspective that the wartime raid was a reality. And, as luck would have it, we are able to look to a second apparently creditable source of corroborative information from Germany, telling essentially the same story.

Chapter 7

The Naval Officer's Tale:
A Second German Perspective

T o have confirmation of a seaborne enemy raid on the Isle of Wight from an impeccable German source, a man who was actually part of the raiding party, is obviously vital to the quest to convert rumours of the landing into historical fact, especially when official records from both sides of the wartime divide are conspicuous by their absence. Yet the story from Dietrich Andernacht is not the only German perspective on the enduring tale. For many years a second narrative has existed, from a man who would appear to be another of the raid's veterans. It is not possible to identify him, but there seems no reason to doubt the underlying truth of his account. Some of the details differ from the Laurence/Andernacht version of the story but, essentially, this second German witness provides corroboration that the raid was a fact. Moreover, his account clearly identifies the radar station at St Lawrence as the raiders' target.

This story comes entirely second-hand. It is therefore again important to consider carefully the conduit through which it has emerged. Fortunately, it flows from an utterly reliable source in the person of Isle of Wight military historian, Gareth Sprack, whose credentials as an informant have recently been underlined by publication of his book, meticulously researched with his wife, Valerie, on the island's own military force, the 8th (Isle of Wight Rifles, Princess Beatrice's) Battalion of the Hampshire Regiment.[1] Despite the fact that he learnt of it several years ago, Gareth's testimony from his meeting with a first-rate German witness to the raid is every bit as compelling and believable as Dietrich Andernacht's own version of the story.

When he met his informant in 1981 and the story was relayed to him, Gareth was not in the least surprised.

'My late father was with the ARP at Shanklin during the war and it was common knowledge in my family that something like this had happened along the Back of the Wight [the local term for the island's south-western coast between the southern tip at St Catherine's Point and The Needles at the isle's western extremity – St Lawrence lies on its fringe, a few miles to the east on the other side of St Catherine's]. It was one of the wartime stories I had grown up with. As a boy, I thought that everyone knew about it. Of course, in a sense we, the generation growing up after the war, fought the Home Front almost as much as our parents had. It was all we heard from them for twenty-five years!'

Gareth was in France when, by chance, he met the man who confirmed the story he repeatedly had heard in the Isle of Wight as a child. In April 1981, as a 'very junior' member of the Fortress Study Group, a prestigious international organisation, registered in the UK, devoted to furthering the understanding of military fortifications, he travelled with his father to join a study tour of fortified areas in eastern France. The itinerary included a look at the 1930s-built Maginot Line of concrete defences, the outer ring of forts at Verdun, scene of a bloody First World War battle between French and German armies in 1916, and some of the many fortifications of the late-nineteenth and early-twentieth centuries encircling the city of Metz near the German border. Thus, the tour's focus was firmly on military defences which pre-dated the Second World War, reflecting Gareth's own particular sphere of interest at the time.

He was in distinguished company. Hosted by a French general of military engineers by the name of Nicolas, the group included the now deceased German army officer Herbert Jager, renowned as an expert on his nation's artillery development between 1860 and 1918, and, probably the best-known in the party, Brigadier Jock Hamilton-Baillie, famed for his numerous escapes from German prisoner of war camps in World War Two. British military authors Christopher F. Foss and Terry Gander were also in this august gathering, together with a number of prominent academics. Gareth recalled:

'People had come from all over Europe to take part in the tour. I remember General Nicolas gave us a very nice lunch in the officers' mess of the engineer regiment to which he was attached. It lasted for five-and-a-half hours!'

General Nicolas clearly did not believe in doing anything by halves.

'He gave us a lecture which went on until half past one in the morning! It was held in the lecture hall of what, looking back, I think was a visitors' centre in Verdun – something like that.'

Bearing in mind thirty-five years had elapsed since the study group's French tour when Gareth spoke of it in 2016, and that some of the details he remembered were bound to be a little hazy, his recall of the trip was impressive – an important consideration in the context of the story he was about to relate.

'I don't believe the gentleman [his German informant] was at the lecture so that makes me wonder whether he was actually part of our tour party. Possibly not because I remember we were in the bar of the hotel we were staying at, the Le Coq Hardi in Verdun, when this elderly gentleman came up to me and my friend, Chris Old. He had obviously heard us speaking in English. "Oh, English!" he said. "Where are you from in England?" I turned round and said, "The Isle of Wight." His eyes lit up and his next words I remember clearly. "Well, I will tell you a story." Of course, thirty-five years have intervened but I think I'm right in saying that's virtually a verbatim account of the first words he said to me.'

The veil over the German's part in the officially unacknowledged wartime incident was lifted. Added Gareth:

'He started to tell his story about the raid and I think he did say it had happened in 1943 when, as I remember it, he had been a young German naval officer. Although he said they had come over in a submarine, I have no recollection that he mentioned they had started out from the Channel Islands. In fact, I would have thought not because I don't believe the Germans used the occupied islands for U-boats. I think it more likely they come across from somewhere else – probably from somewhere along the French coast.'

The reference by Alfred Laurence to Alderney, and the Channel Islands in general, as a 'launch-pad' for the raid had raised eyebrows, especially among the islands' historians, groups such as the Channel Islands Occupation Society in Guernsey and the Alderney Society, who have delved deeply into the minutiae of the German occupation years. They had pointed out that the islands had no facilities for harbouring submarines and implied that it was far more likely any U-boat crossing the Channel on a mission to the Isle of Wight would have set out from the nearest purpose-built submarine pens on the Brittany coast at Brest. The direct journey northeast to the south coast of Wight would have skirted the Alderney shoreline before the Channel crossing of a little over seventy miles began in earnest. This seems the simplest explanation for the suggested Alderney link. Possibly it was from here, the most northerly of the Channel Islands, that the U-boat was submerged for its mission. Maybe it was off the island the raiding party clambered aboard the sub from their dinghies.

Given the length of time that had elapsed since 1943, its effect on people's memories and the obvious susceptibility to misinterpretation and confusion which bedevils all oft-repeated stories in their telling and re-telling, it was not surprising that some of the details between the two German accounts – as with those emanating from the Isle of Wight –were inconsistent. 'The whole story has become so convoluted that some people seem to believe the Germans were landed by E-boat,' added Gareth. 'That was certainly not the story that was related to me.'

It must surely be regarded as a safe bet that the voyage was made in a submarine. Gareth continued:

'Having made the crossing, the U-boat then lay off the Isle of Wight coast, submerged in St Catherine's Deep, for twenty-four hours, allowing things to settle down. The plan was for the sub to pop up at a time which would coincide with virtually every E-boat on the other side of the English Channel dashing about and doing all sorts of things to distract everybody from Dover to Cornwall. Having a lot of distraction was vital to the plan for the raid.'

Distraction, of course, was the measure employed by the British – though in the shape of its air force rather than its navy – to dispel enemy suspicion on the night of the Bruneval raid in 1942. The possibility of major E-boat distraction on the night of the following year's attack on RAF St Lawrence's radar station can only be addressed with the aid of British records if it is possible to pinpoint the precise or, at the very least, probable date of the German operation, an unsurprisingly problematic issue, examined in chapter 8, which follows many a twist and turn.

The former Kriegsmarine officer told Gareth the raiders came ashore in rubber dinghies.

'He was in command of a dinghy containing five men. Apart from himself, two of them were German soldiers, there to defend, and the other two were technicians – to do whatever it was at the radar station they had come over to do. I have always assumed they used only the one dinghy to come ashore, but he might have meant he was in charge of one dinghy among others.'

Apparently credible evidence exists to suggest that at least two dinghies were used for the raid – ferrying a probable total of ten men to the beach (see chapter 8). But where did the German party come ashore? Had Gareth's informant specifically mentioned their target?

'Yes, he had. He said it was St Lawrence – the radar station. He was certain. That's virtually a clincher for me. How the hell would a German know about St Lawrence, a tiny village on the Isle of Wight, unless he had very good reason to remember it?'

In 1940, in addition to numerous other defensive obstacles, the island had been ringed with an anti-invasion barrier which it was hoped would at least hinder any attempt at a large-scale mechanised assault on the local beaches. This was an obvious move, especially in Sandown Bay, on the eastern shoreline. German invasion had appeared imminent. Indeed, prior to the drawing-up of the final invasion plans for Hitler's eventually aborted *Unternehmen Seelöwe* (Operation Sea Lion), the bay had for an extended period been regarded by the Germans as a potential target. On 16 July, following the fall of France, his forces' capture of the Channel Islands and, to his fury, the refusal of Britain to capitulate, Hitler had decreed in a Führer Directive that 'the landing [in England] will be in the form of a surprise crossing on a wide front from about Ramsgate to the area west of the Isle of Wight …'.

Added the Führer, 'The possible advantages of limited operations before the general crossing (e.g. the occupation of the Isle of Wight or of the county of Cornwall) are to be considered'. Hitler did not, of course, share his intentions with the British, but Wight's vulnerability to attack was clear. Although St Lawrence did not acquire its very obvious, highly susceptible clifftop radar station until 1942, two years after the island's anti-invasion barrier was installed by garrison troops, the relative ease of access offered at Woody Bay to a potential enemy force, perhaps seeking a landing site to supplement a principal assault a few miles to the northeast in Sandown Bay, ensured that this stretch of the coastline was not left out of the barrier.

Yet, while the barrier, constructed principally of scaffolding, might have proved an effective deterrent to the landing of enemy tanks, it would not significantly have hampered a band of lightly-armed raiders. They would simply have climbed over it. Neither in the Laurence/Andernacht story, nor in the tale recounted to Gareth Sprack is any mention made of a barrier, or any other form of fixed beach defence, presenting a troublesome hindrance to the German force. Similarly, their reported use of lightweight inflatable craft on the approach to the shore would significantly have limited the risk of negotiating the probable presence of mines.

But Gareth's informant confirmed that, once ashore, the raiders ran into trouble.

'They had been briefed that they would more than likely meet Home Guard [on defence duties at the radar station] but they didn't – they met regular soldiers. He didn't tell me exactly who these men were but my vague memory is that they might have been from either the Duke of Cornwall's Light Infantry or the Somerset Light Infantry. I'm sure it was one of the light infantry regiments. Anyway, it wasn't incident-free. There was a firefight, though it was only brief.'

On the face of it, this reference to the possible identity of the British troops on guard duty at St Lawrence at the time of the raid should be a key piece of information in determining the date the assault took place. If Dietrich Andernacht was correct in suggesting an assault in May 1943, the infantry component of the 17,000-strong Isle of Wight military garrison, augmented by two Home Guard battalions, would have been in the hands of the 214th Independent Infantry Brigade, part of the British Army's 43rd Wessex Division. Composed of newly-raised battalions from English infantry regiments, the brigade had assumed beach defence duties on the island in January 1941 following departure of the original defensive force provided by the 12th Infantry Brigade in the wake of the 1940 evacuation of the British Expeditionary Force from Dunkirk. Since November 1942 the 214th had been commanded by Brigadier Hubert Essame, its composition subject to frequent change.

In May 1943 both the Duke of Cornwall's Light Infantry and the Somerset Light Infantry were represented in 214th Brigade by single territorial battalions. The 5th DCLI had been stationed on the island since August 1942, the 7th SLI arriving a month later. Initially, the two battalions had linked up with the Wiltshire Regiment's 7th Battalion to form 214th Brigade but records indicate the 7th Wilts were quickly replaced by the Devonshire Regiment's 12th Battalion. In the context of the defence of beaches in the Ventnor area during the spring of 1943, the spotlight falls directly on the Somerset Light Infantry, the 7th Battalion having assumed responsibility for the island's south sector defences on 8 January, headquartered in the town. According to the regimental history, they remained at Ventnor until leaving the isle with the rest of the brigade on 27 May – the only date in the month concerning the 7th Battalion referred to in the official history.[2] Within a few days a sub-district formation under the aegis of the 47th (London) Infantry Division had arrived on the island to take on the beach defence role.

So, if the attack did take place in May, and it *was* soldiers from the 7th Somerset Light Infantry who fought the German landing party at St Lawrence, the raid would have to have happened before the 27th of that month. The fact that regimental records compiled after the war appear to throw absolutely no light on the matter would not be surprising if a permanent clampdown on revealing anything about the assault has been applied. Is it possible to look elsewhere?

Would the 7th SLI's war diary, the battalion's contemporary day-by-day record of its Isle of Wight posting, be more illuminating? A search for this has proved elusive. While the Somerset Heritage Centre, the county's record office in Taunton, holds an extensive archival collection for the regiment as a whole, there seems to be nothing of direct relevance to the 7th Battalion's service on the island with 214th Infantry Brigade The Somerset Military Museum in the county town has proved the main source of information relating to the 7th SLI but its suggested cross-reference to the National Archives at Kew for war diary records has proved fruitless. Is any of this suspicious – or even relevant? Once more the obvious need to determine, as near as possible, from other sources the probable date of the assault is drawn into focus – something more fully explored in the context of archival examination in chapter 8.

Whatever the make-up of the army's guard troops at St Lawrence when the Germans landed there, the outcome of the short exchange of fire, according to Gareth Sprack's informant, was a loss of life, a detail seemingly at odds with the Laurence/Andernacht version of events. Gareth continued:

'As I understood it, two Brits were killed and one of the Germans, possibly one of the men in this guy's dinghy, was seriously wounded. Of course, he might have been referring here solely to the details of a firefight relating to the men in his particular boat. I can't remember now exactly how he described it but I do recall him mentioning those two British casualties and the one German who was injured and who, he said, died on the way back.

'I don't remember him saying anything about the taking of British prisoners. He simply told me, "we got what we wanted," and I have always understood that to mean pieces of radar equipment. I've heard since that some people think they also pinched the actual radar technicians at the station but I have to say I have no recollection of that from the story he told me.'

It would, of course, have made sense from the German point of view for them to have captured a technician, possibly more than one, just as Johnny Frost's paras had done at Bruneval in 1942, but this may be nothing more than speculation on the part of post-war purveyors of the story in Britain, and particularly on the Isle of Wight. There are a great many local variations to the 'basic' tale of a German landing. Among these is a story that one of the raiders escaped the firefight but, instead of returning to the U-boat with his colleagues, remained on the island for some days in hiding until virtual starvation forced him to surrender to either the military or civilian authorities. The tale's source has long been lost in the mist of time.

As an aside to this, based on the recorded evidence of one British veteran, it is tempting, though possibly mischievous, to wonder whether a German serviceman, even one dressed in uniform, would have been recognised as such around Ventnor in wartime. Robert Neilands' 2004 work for Pen & Sword Books, *By Land & By Sea: The Story of the Royal Marine Commandos*, included recollections from Charles (Jim) McNeill who in 1942 was billeted among a detachment of men from 40 RM Commando at Ventnor. McNeill recalled that 'life on the island was pretty good, but the locals weren't very observant. One day the CO got some men to dress up in German uniforms and walk about the town – but nobody even noticed!'

Gareth Sprack's story from his chance encounter in France more than three decades ago may be second-hand but its route to the surface is markedly more direct than most of the rumours which have been told and re-told down the years about the legendary 'raid on the radar'. Its ultimate source, despite the drawback of its anonymity, places it on a par with the Laurence/ Andernacht version in terms of believability. It is a pity that Gareth cannot identify his informant by name but, to be fair, events in the 1939–45 war held no particular fascination for him as a young man touring fortifications from earlier conflicts.

'I can't precisely remember my mind-set at the time but to me World War Two was far too modern – it didn't really interest me!'

Neither had the tale recounted to him by the former German naval officer in 1981 come as an earth-shattering revelation.

'No, as I said, it didn't come as a surprise to me at all. I mean, this guy basically had only confirmed what my dad had told me when I was a small boy. As far as I was concerned back then, there really was no big deal about it – end of story!'

To his credit, however, it did occur to Gareth to ask the German veteran a question which shrieks out to this day from those who are told the gist of the fabled raid story. The British may have had good reason for keeping the story quiet on initial grounds of security and national morale – before the secret apparently became a habit, for whatever reason, which was never intended to be broken – but why on earth has nothing emerged officially from Germany about this apparently successful daredevil operation right under the nose of an enemy?

The ex-serviceman had told his story as if he were letting the fizz out of a long-closed bottle of pop. 'Surely,' asked Gareth, 'this incident would be in your national archives, wouldn't it?'

'Almost certainly not,' the man replied. 'Your Intelligence people had done a very good job'. He had apparently been told by someone he knew, a man who appeared to have been speaking with an air of relevant authority, that, on capturing German documentation immediately after the war, British agents – Gareth thought he specifically mentioned Naval Intelligence – had spent several years carrying out a thorough 'weeding' job to find anything of general interest to the UK and, at the same time, remove from the future record what was considered to be embarrassing or otherwise unsuitable for dissemination among the British public.

Gareth Sprack, for one, is very open to this possibility:

'I was once doing some research at the Imperial War Museum's film archive, discussing the practicalities of restoring old footage. They were telling me that one of the things they have to go through on discovering "new" film is to "weed it to make sure there is nothing on there that we don't want people to see." I said, "Surely these things can't still be military secrets!" He replied, "Oh no, it's just that, well, for example, we don't want people to see a photograph of a prominent military figure holding hands with a schoolboy, or something like that!" That's why they're weeding things – it's to protect the reputation of well-known historical personalities. Well, that was certainly the impression they gave me, anyway. Perhaps in the case of the German raid the UK authorities are again protecting reputations and long-accepted national pronouncements. The British are particularly good at keeping things secret, probably better than most other nations.'

A battle-scarred country emerging victorious from a prolonged threat by the forces of evil to its very existence as a proud, independent democratic state might be excused for not drawing attention to an embarrassing, if ultimately not far-reaching, blemish on its record of home soil impregnability. This is an arguable point, of course, but it is not hard to understand why Winston Churchill might have wanted to keep a successful mid-war enemy raid on the Isle of Wight a secret long after hostilities had finally ceased. After all, in the grand scheme of things, what did it really matter? The island was not captured; it was not that sort of operation. It was a jolt, worrying at the time, but there was no need to dwell on it; no need to acknowledge it at all. As the German Jewish philosopher Walter Benjamin put it, 'history is written by the victors'.

If this reasoning did apply, as Gareth Sprack's informant claimed, in the context of captured German records of the seaborne raid he described – and there is obviously a need to regard such a suggestion cautiously with only the barest of hearsay evidence to base it on – it would certainly help to explain the absence of formal post-war recognition in Germany. But this would still leave a baffling mystery, arguably the greatest of the many imponderables in the whole story. If the raid was a reality and the raiders achieved their objective, why did the Germans apparently make no use of this as an important piece of propaganda in 1943? It would surely have been regarded as a gift, a golden nugget for the traitorous Fascist broadcaster William Joyce – Lord Haw-Haw to his mocking British audience – as he delivered his nightly dose of Nazi misinformation in his notorious *Germany Calling* radio slot. Indeed, while he might have been expected to embellish the story with wildly exaggerated claims, in essence Joyce would not even have been required to make it up!

In *Silencing Lord Haw-Haw: An analysis of British public reaction to the broadcasts, conviction and execution of Nazi propagandist William Joyce*, published online in 2015 by Western Oregon University, US writer Matthew Rock Cahill observed that, 'by 1943 few in Great Britain bothered to listen to anything he had to say'.[3] This is undeniably true. The initial novelty of tuning in to this self-proclaimed British-Irish patriot's darkly mischievous outpourings had worn off. For many, Lord Haw-Haw had become something more akin to Lord Bore-Bore. Yet, he was still 'calling from Germany' in 1943 and it is difficult to imagine him looking this particularly bountiful gift horse in the mouth. If he did refer to it, the recording of the relevant broadcast appears not to have survived among the archival collection preserved, among others, by the BBC.[4]

Interestingly, according to one source, Joyce did refer in his broadcasts to a landing by German troops on the English south coast – but claimed it was in Kent. In his memoirs, Geoff Young, a private in the Wiltshire Regiment's 4th Battalion, a Territorial Army unit, described a strange incident while the battalion was guarding a section of the Kent coast at Kingsdown beach, Deal.

'It was while we were here that one of our soldiers suddenly disappeared whilst on sentry duty. The idea that he had just deserted would have been completely out of character for him. But missing he was and the affair remained a mystery until Lord Haw-Haw … announced in one of his broadcasts that a soldier – he actually named him – of the 4th Wilts had been captured and was now a prisoner of war in Germany. It was later confirmed that a German E-boat had landed a snatch party at Kingsdown, intent on taking a prisoner.'

We have no precise date for this curious story, which bears obvious similarities to the various accounts described earlier of soldiers being taken captive by German raiders on the Isle of Wight, although it was clearly during an early period of the war, some years before the 4th Wilts joined the Allied assault on Normandy in the weeks following the initial D-Day landings in June 1944.[5] There appear to be no other references to the story recalled by the former soldier. It is therefore hard to know what to make of it, especially as it relies to an extent on the ultra-unreliability of a William Joyce broadcast. We may conjecture, however, that if the Germans were capable of successfully carrying out a raid on St Lawrence radar station, they may well have repeated the deed, or something similar, elsewhere along the coast.

That thought had clearly occurred to Gareth Sprack when he met his German informant in the Verdun hotel bar back in 1981.

'I asked him if he had done any more of these raids. He replied that, personally, he hadn't been on any others but added that there were always rumours that the Germans were carrying out other raids apart from the one he was involved with.'

If William Joyce did refer to the capture of a soldier in Kent, the chances are it would have been written off by most of his radio audience as a typical piece of malevolent propaganda. It does not seem unreasonable to suppose that, if he also bragged about a successful German raid on the Isle of Wight, or anywhere else in Britain, that too would have received short shrift.

But what of the apparent deaths of the British defenders at St Lawrence, outlined to Gareth Sprack. Several questions arise. How could the German raiders be sure the soldiers had been killed? Would they have waited around long enough to confirm the fatalities? This seems unlikely though the possibility of course exists that, if the soldiers were shot at point-blank range, their deaths might well have been obvious. The bigger questions around this are equally obvious. If there were British fatalities, were the details of their funerals and probable inquests supressed by the UK authorities as part of an overall cover-up of the facts? And where were they buried? Has this information similarly been wiped from the slate of wartime history?

There is obviously a need to examine the possibilities arising from this conundrum in a search for clarification, should any exist. For reasons connected with an apparent disparity over the probable date of the raid – set out in chapter 8 – it is better to delay this task until later.

Considering the total lack at the time of writing of any nationally archived documentation in either Britain or Germany, evidential reliability is obviously crucially important in trying to piece together the various aspects of the 'raid on the radar' legend from the sources which do exist. Dietrich Andernacht's credentials would seem to be impeccable, but how reliable as a witness was the former German naval officer? Gareth Sprack recalled:

'As I remember it, in later life he was something to do with the University of Heidelberg [founded in 1386 at Baden-Württemberg, the oldest university in contemporary Germany and the fifth oldest in central Europe]. When I went to Heidelberg several years later it was always in the back of my mind – that must be where that guy came from. He may well have been an academic. If he was on our tour, and as I have said I don't know that he was, he must have had at least a passing interest in military history. Or maybe he was simply in the Verdun area at the time to look at the old fortifications. He certainly did not come across as a travelling shoe salesman, if I can put it that way!'

It would be foolishly presumptuous to accept without question this assessment of the former German officer's character and reliability as an informant but, on the face of it, the impression he made on Gareth Sprack in 1981 firmly suggests he was, like Andernacht, a man unlikely to have been in the habit of making up wild stories about his wartime experiences. Notwithstanding the apparent disparity in some of the details between the two men's recollections, their stories, once stripped down, are basically the same. To regard this as coincidence, to suggest that two seemingly erudite, rational ex-servicemen with no apparent post-war connection would around the same time independently invent a fib of such grandiose proportions in order to seek attention, amusement or whatever is surely wide of the mark.[6]

Chapter 8

Archival Fishing: Trawling the Local Sources

I f a German raiding force did land on the Isle of Wight in 1943 it seemed a reasonable assumption that, despite the apparent official cover-up, some accessible documentary evidence might yet have survived in the UK to prove, or at least strongly support the view, that it had happened. This would mean it had somehow escaped the governmental censorship which seemed to have airbrushed this symbolically significant event very effectively from the British historical record. Dietrich Andernacht had provided a key pointer to the likely date – probably sometime in May – but how reliable would this turn out to be? And from where might there be some reliable, yet apparently forgotten, contemporary British reference to his, and Gareth Sprack's 1981 German naval informant's, daring wartime adventure on the island?

There was, in fact, a good chance that such information might be readily available on the Isle of Wight itself among the operational diaries of the island's Air Raid Precautions service. These recorded in some detail not only the large number of air raids which, directly or indirectly, had affected the island between June 1940 and November 1944, but also a catalogue of other events which had impacted on the ARP's work throughout that period of the war.

Would this illuminating contemporary record of wartime incidents, preserved intact at the Isle of Wight Record Office in Newport[1], shed some light on the legendary raid, an event that, if it really did take place, would surely not have been ignored, at least up to a permitted point, by the island's civil defence authority? True, any mention of the raid, if raid there was, in the diaries had escaped my attention during a read-through for earlier research into the island's war. On the other hand, I had not been alerted to the rumours at that time and might well have missed possibly 'submerged' references to an enemy landing. It was worth a try.

Following the Andernacht lead, the ARP records for May 1943 were consulted first. Disappointingly, there was nothing that could be linked to a German raid, nor indeed to anything of major importance in the area of Ventnor. But Dr Andernacht had been vague about the date. Maybe it had happened in June. The ARP record for that month was full of references to a German attack in the south of the island – but this was the well-documented tip and run raid which, as recounted in chapter 3, narrowly missed the radar station at RAF Blackgang. There was no hint of a seaborne raid. Could it have been in July? Again, the record failed to provide a shred of corroborative evidence in support of the seaborne raid story.

Was the August record even worth a look? Could Andernacht have been this far out with his timing? Yet it seemed pointless to abandon the search at this stage. People's memories are prone to fallibility – especially after a span of several decades. August was still in the summer of 1943. It would not really be that surprising if Frankfurt's former archivist's recollection was three months adrift. However, with a perusal of the month's ARP record fast approaching the midway point, and with still no hint of a German raid, hopes were starting to fade.

A suspected enemy aircraft in the sea off St Lawrence overnight on 12–13 August at least brought the relevant area into focus, but was probably of little significance. The ARP record for three nights later, however, was a different story altogether. The enemy on the night of 15–16 August was in robust action. Portsmouth had been targeted by the Luftwaffe. Chaos reigned in the city – and it seemed it was on this Sunday night, with attention focussed across the Solent, that a small German raiding force may have sneaked into the waters south of the Isle of Wight.

The air raid was the heaviest attack on Portsmouth for more than a year and the last in the war to cause high numbers of casualties there. It began soon after midnight when a *pfadfinder* (pathfinder) force of Dornier Do-217s from the 1./KG66 northern French base at Montdidier,[2] flying in over Selsey Bill, turned west to drop strings of multi-coloured flares and target indicators, followed by large numbers of incendiaries, as spectacular illumination for a following formation of bombers, attached to sister unit 3./KG66, to unleash a deadly deluge of high-explosive bombs on the city and its dockyard. British estimates of the total number of aircraft involved vary considerably – from twenty-five in some locally published accounts to ninety-one! It is probable that the lower estimate refers only to the strength of the pathfinder force.

It should be noted that there is some dispute over the exact composition of the Luftwaffe formation. While virtually all reports refer solely to the use of 217s in both parts of the attack, some sources suggest the force included aircraft from 3./KG2, which had been moved from Gilze-en Rijen airfield in the southern Netherlands to the forward base of Dreux in northern France, from where the 217s joined the overnight attack on Portsmouth. Across the Solent, the Isle of Wight did not entirely escape the wrath of this fearsome enemy offensive. Watching the spectacle from Ryde, which lies directly opposite the city in the island's northeast, a 36-year-old woman was killed when a rocket shell struck the town's All Saints Church.

The Portsmouth area's anti-aircraft guns probably accounted for two of the enemy force while a third crashed on fire at the entrance to Portsmouth Harbour. A fourth plane, attacked by an RAF Mosquito night-fighter while attempting to get away, plummeted in flames into the sea south of the Isle of Wight. At the ARP post in Ventnor there was confusion. At first it seemed another aircraft had crashed into the Channel off the local coast. Later, at 1.23, the town's ARP wardens received reports that the sighting had actually been of flares rather than a plane – but this was to prove the precursor to a night of high drama in the far south of the island.

Just over an hour later, at 2.30, the ARP's island headquarters at Newport was alerted to a startling development. The diary entry compiled by the HQ staff on duty was stark: 'Special Report,' it read. 'Police report two dinghies full of Germans in sea off Ventnor. Seen at 2.18 … reported to police through navy.' According to the ARP record, the dramatic message was relayed immediately to 'Group Intelligence', a probable reference to higher authority at the organisation's national headquarters in Slough, Bucks. Minutes later, events took another turn in Ventnor when the local ARP post received a report from the wartime National Fire Service.

It came at 2.40: 'NFS reports fire near pylons at Ventnor. Two pumps are attending with it.' Was this linked to the apparent German presence in the area? At that stage there would have been no way of knowing, and, anyway, Ventnor ARP had not yet been notified of the seemingly sinister dinghies.

But the ARP Officer's mention of 'the pylons at Ventnor' had brought the area's radar installations sharply into focus on the overnight canvas – and this was almost certainly a reference, mistakenly or not, to the Chain Home station on St Boniface Down.

Unsurprisingly, the main thrust of ARP messaging related to be the sighting of the enemy off the coast. At 2.42 the worrying news was relayed to the Ventnor post from Newport HQ. The scant details were essentially unchanged except for a three-minute amendment to the time the enemy had been spotted – changed from 2.18 to 2.15. That was of minor significance, of course; the essential message was that the Germans were apparently in the vicinity of Ventnor and the town's ARP wardens should 'observe usual precautions in case they should land'.

And that, frustratingly, was that. There were no further references in the Isle of Wight's ARP record to the enemy sighting, how it was dealt with and by whom. While the message from Newport had assumed the Germans were spotted on their arrival in local waters, and not as they attempted to depart, the diary shed no real light on this and provided absolutely no clue as to the purpose, outcome or repercussions of the overnight visit. It was never mentioned again.

Did the German party land? If so, precisely where and what was their objective? How was the Royal Navy (presumably in the form of a patrolling vessel although naval archives preserved today at Portsmouth shed no light on this) so sure they *were* Germans? How many men were in the dinghies? Does this mysterious incident tie in with the rumoured raid on a radar station? Based on this evidence alone, there are clearly more questions than answers. Yet, the ARP record did seem to support the contention that an enemy force, albeit one probably composed of limited numbers, had reached the Isle of Wight in 1943 on active service.

Why else would they have been there? As noted, German aircraft were shot down on that eventful night and, on the face of it at least, it is not inconceivable that the men seen off Ventnor were Luftwaffe aircrew who had survived the death throes of their plane, probably in flames, and ended up in the sea. But it is clear they were spotted together in rubber dinghies. From where could these craft have come to aid stricken airmen? If there were two dinghies – and there might have been others if they had managed to evade the watchful eyes of the Royal Navy – this would indicate a minimum of ten men, possibly more. Dornier 217s normally carried a crew of four. Only the one Do-217 reportedly came down in the sea anywhere near the southern Isle of Wight coast. While the 217s were equipped with dinghy storage, located in heavily protected casing above the two rear bomb cells in the centre section of the fuselage, this provided space for just a single inflatable. The ARP reports clearly refer to dinghies in the plural. There is, however, some indication that enemy aircrew *were* plucked from the sea south of the island that night – though the evidence is somewhat hazy.

Understandably, errors were sometimes made by those employed on wartime plane-spotting duties in the UK. This was clearly the case on the Isle of Wight overnight on 15–16 August 1943. The Royal Observer Corps spotters' post in the centre of the island at Mount Joy, Newport, recorded the shooting down of 'five hostiles' (enemy planes) during the raid on Portsmouth. Surviving ROC documentation suggests that the crew of one of these aircraft were rescued by a Walrus amphibious bi-plane 'off St Catherine's Point'. This would seem to be a reference to the Dornier which other accounts describe as coming down in flames five miles south of Niton – the village closest to St Catherine's. However, the ROC report confuses things by referring to the aircraft as a Heinkel He-111, almost certainly a spotter's error. More importantly, there appears to be no other record of its crew being rescued from the sea.

A leading source of information among the wartime plane spotters, H.J.T. (Jock) Leal, studiously chronicled details of the air war above the Isle of Wight for two books, initially published in 1982 and 1988 respectively by the *Isle of Wight County Press* in Newport. In the first of these *Air War over the Island*, he wrote that 'five German planes were shot down, one in the St Catherine's area,' during the August 1943 attack, adding that 'the crew bailed out and were seen in a rubber dinghy south of Niton'. Leal did not mention a subsequent air-sea rescue, providing no further information on the ultimate fate of the airmen, their identity or that of their doomed aircraft. Recalling the 'short, sharp' raid in his more comprehensive second book, *Battle in the Skies over the Isle of Wight*, the former observer, amending his earlier narrative after consulting with other sources, referred only to the burning Dornier crashing into the sea five miles off Niton, adding nothing further about the incident except to explain that, while every effort had been made to obtain full details of the Do-217s and their crews brought down in the attack, nothing had come to light.

We are left with a mystery. These scant, somewhat conflicting details again throw up more questions than answers. Did the four-man Dornier crew really escape their stricken aircraft several miles off the Isle of Wight coast? Was it really these men who were seen in a rubber dinghy? Were they really at the centre of an air-sea rescue? Or were the wartime plane spotters led astray on that memorable night by a German raid of an altogether different nature? We might also ask – have their subsequent accounts fallen prey to murky British fudge?

There is, potentially at least, another possible explanation for the presence of 'dinghies full of Germans' in the coastal waters off the island. Might they have been survivors of a shipwreck? While this sounds an entirely plausible theory, there are no records whatsoever in support of it.

If we are to conclude that the reported German dinghies were not linked in any way to either a plane crash or a shipping calamity, as seems most probably the case, the likelihood that the inflatables were instead spotted in the act of ferrying a party of enemy raiders either to or from a seaborne assault dramatically increases. So were they coming or going when seen by the Royal Navy at 2.15 on the Sunday morning? Neither Dietrich Andernacht nor Gareth Sprack's naval informant had provided a specific time for the raid. From both there was merely the detail that, unsurprisingly, it had been a night raid. It seems, however, that Alfred Laurence had hinted at a more specific period of time in conversation with the island's then archaeological officer, David Tomalin, about the story he had heard from Dr Andernacht.

'He told [Dr Tomalin] that, when the two were chatting in Germany, the conversation had turned to the Isle of Wight. His friend mentioned that he had been on the Isle of Wight during the war! Obviously surprised by this, Laurence inquired about the circumstances. "I was part of a U-boat mission which carried out a raid there," the friend [Amdernacht] replied. "We had to leave at first light and we managed it – we never saw them [the British] again that night."'

Sunrise on the Isle of Wight in mid-August would now normally be just before six o'clock. If the ARP record from 15–16 August 1943 does relate to the raid, and the reference by Dr Andernacht to a 'first light' getaway has been correctly passed on, it would follow that the 2.15 sighting of the dinghies must have been at the time of the raiders' imminent arrival on the island rather than their departure up to three-and-a-half hours later (though by then the clocks in Britain would have been turned back an hour at 3am as the wartime daylight saving procedure changed from Double DST, two hours ahead of standard time, to DST, one hour ahead). If this was the case, it is a further matter for conjecture how much of a surprise an enemy landing that night at RAF St Lawrence would have been. Was the station alerted to the threat?[3]

At the lighthouse on St Catherine's Point, which had very quickly been put back in action after the 1 June tip and run raid described in chapter 3, the keepers' log book, preserved on site, provides another contemporary record of events on the island's southern coast during the dramatic night of 15–16 August 1943. As the Luftwaffe battered Portsmouth, the keepers recorded air raid warnings at 1.22 (the 'all clear' following at 1.35) and then at 1.44 (with the 'all clear' at 2.23). Throughout this period – indeed, between 11pm on the 15th and 3.05 in the morning – the log book reveals that the St Catherine's light was shown at 'reduced brilliance'. As the keepers' log makes clear, reducing the brilliance of the beam was frequently ordered, the usual reason being to provide a degree of guidance to a friendly convoy of ships entering or leaving home waters without running too great a risk of alerting a watchful enemy to its presence. It is arguable whether this would significantly have hindered a clandestine approach across the Channel by a seaborne raiding force – or, conversely, would actually have increased its opportunity to sneak in to the local coast without being seen.

Whether the decision to reduce the St Catherine's beam in the early hours of 16 August 1943 points to prior knowledge that an enemy incursion was likely, or at least possible, is a further argument. With very little in the way of hard evidence to support such a proposition, it is probably unwise to read too much into the order – issued at 8.30pm on the 15th – to dim the light.

If the raid did take place on the night of 15–16 August 1943, was there any evidence relating to that night of the major distraction tactics Gareth

Sprack's German informant suggested were employed by the enemy's naval forces? If this was the case, it seems to have escaped the notice of Peter C. Smith in writing his superb book, *Naval Warfare in the English Channel 1939–45*, published in 2007 by Pen & Sword Books. He mentions no activity to speak of at all in the Channel that night. Maybe the answer to this is that the German craft had actually diverted attention a long way from the Channel – perhaps as far as the Atlantic – in a bid to allow the raiding party the quietest of approaches to their target. Evidence is lacking but, as a tactic, distraction at sea, in addition to the air raid on Portsmouth, certainly would have made sense.

Raid folklore on the island is usually vague about the precise date of the German incursion. It would obviously be of immense value to uncover further evidence tying the story to that August night. Was there anybody who could provide this? Fortunately, there was. In March 2015, an 89-year-old man's precise recall of events in the period which immediately preceded his military call-up added persuasive verbal testimony to the incomplete official record of the ARP.

Derek Kent was carrying out duties for the ARP as a teenage dispatch rider, based at Shanklin Town Hall, when rumours began to filter through that the Germans had raided the island.

'We heard about it when we were sent to the St Lawrence and Niton area. We were also told of the rumours when we went up to the pylons [RAF Ventnor] on St Boniface Down. They said the Germans had been spotted out to sea off St Lawrencee – I'm not sure at what point. This must have been around 16 August 1943. On the 17th, so just a day later, a man dressed in a suit came down to see us with Mr Dunkinson, who was in charge of our ARP.

'Harold Brennan, another dispatch rider who has since died, and I were asked to sign the Official Secrets Act, which meant that we couldn't reveal any sensitive information. I don't remember the man saying too much more. He just told me I had to sign because I had just turned eighteen, but I have often thought since that he might have been deliberately vague as "cover". We were taken into the telephone room at the town hall to sign. There were women telephonists there.

Perhaps they had to sign the Act too – I don't know – but the date has always stuck in my mind because it was just after my birthday. I joined the army soon after that.'

Derek Kent's recollections do not, of course, confirm conclusively that a raid took place. He did not see any Germans land. Neither did he see any leave. Yet his clear recall of the date he was 'invited' to sign the Official Secrets Act, and the probability that it was the day after he was told of a rumoured enemy raid, reinforces the case that a seaborne German force was poised to land, or did in fact land, on the Isle of Wight coast in the early hours of 16 August 1943.

It is worth noting that most local tales of the supposed raid conclude with the assertion that, immediately following it, anybody on the island who had either witnessed it or been told of it was visited by the archetypal 'man from the Ministry' and made to sign the Official Secrets Act.

There is another reason for pursuing the night of 15–16 August 1943 as the most probable date for the German operation. Alfred Laurence's reference to the raiders taking away 'a broadcasting or emission device' from the RAF station begs the question – what exactly could this have been? A possible answer to this may be the CRDF (cathode ray direction finding) equipment which was certainly considered for use at St Lawrence during the summer of 1943 and might well have been installed there on a trial basis before the station was apparently ruled out as a suitable location for it. CRDF's ability to provide instantaneous direction indication (later used to good effect against Hitler's V-weapons) would clearly have interested the Germans who might well have seized the chance to snatch an example in August.

Whether or not the apparently enforced post-incident secrecy wholly succeeded during the latter part of that month in covering up the rumours of a raid is a moot point. It appears that stories of an enemy landing were very soon circulating freely in the Isle of Wight – though this might have happened immediately afterwards, before an official clampdown was imposed. 'You heard rumours at the time that the Germans had landed,' recalled Patricia Morgan, who worked at Ryde, in the island's northeast, but lived at Shanklin, several miles' closer to the south coast radar stations. 'Of course, everybody pooh-poohed the stories,' she added.

John Woodford clearly remembered stories of an enemy incursion while at school in Ryde. 'We heard that the Germans had landed in the south of the island,' he said. 'It must have been around 1942 or 1943.' Again, his recall of the approximate period in the war the rumours were circulating is important in that it distinguishes the tale from the many circulating in 1940.

Gareth Sprack's wife, Val, recalled hearing from her father, Ted Cotton, about his experiences as a Home Guard in the rural Shorwell and Brighstone area close to the island's south-western shoreline.

'He said that one evening, when they were doing the harvest, which would have been about August, he was sent out with his rifle onto the cliff at Atherfield holiday camp because there was a lot of activity in the Channel and they were convinced the Germans were going to land.'

Val was unable to say what happened next but it is possibly worth bearing in mind that Atherfield Point is less than ten miles to the northwest from St Lawrence radar site at Woody Bay, If this story relates to 1943, it suggests that the isle had been alerted to a possible enemy raid.

It is, however, right to add that rumours of mid-war German incursions on the Isle of Wight (as was the case elsewhere) were sometimes sparked by a simple misreading of a situation entirely devoid of sinister overtones. A good example of this came in 1973, when a former soldier recalled a somewhat inglorious episode of his war service as part of the 214th Independent Infantry Brigade stationed in the island on beach defensive duties from January 1941.

Philip Davis had arrived with the 19th Battalion of the Royal Fusiliers, which helped to make up the brigade, and was based at Northcourt, the Jacobean manor house on the edge of Shorwell village.

'One night in June 1941 I was on guard duty in the grounds. Part of my patrol was along that side of the house which was skirted by a stream. I was enjoying the sound of the water and the stillness of the night when I heard a bell ringing. We had been warned that an invasion would be heralded by a ringing of church bells. Thinking this was it, I called out the guard commander, who turned out the guard. The duty officer arrived in pyjamas and sweater and rang brigade HQ [based outside Newport town centre].

'Brigade knew nothing of this and were about to set further wheels in motion when the duty officer had the brilliant idea of ringing the Vicar of Shorwell who, after all, should have known why the bells were being rung. We were somewhat abashed to learn from him that, when the wind was in a certain direction on a still night, one could hear the bell buoy off the coast at the nearby village of Brighstone. The alert was cancelled and I was distinctly unpopular!'[4]

Closely mirroring similar wartime tales from coastal locations throughout the UK, stories such as this one, entertaining though they are, inevitably serve to muddy the waters of historical research – especially when that research is mired already in a deep pool of intrigue. They add greatly to the folklore but the need to distinguish these tales from the core quest is clear.

The ARP diary from 15–16 August 1943, while admittedly incomplete and open to interpretation, carried the obvious distinction of being a written contemporary record, something otherwise very hard to find in seeking out the truth of the 'raid on the radar' legend. In searching for other documented evidence, a trawl through archived wartime copies of the Isle of Wight's local press was highly unlikely to yield much, if anything, of relevance to a seaborne German raid, irrespective of whether or not there had been a specific cover-up.

While air raids on an island town in which a newspaper was published could be, and were, reported, the precise identity of the target area was always highly generalised owing to strict wartime censorship. 'A raid on a south coast town' was usually about as much as the censor would allow journalists to reveal, although it would of course have been obvious to readers precisely which town had been attacked. An enemy air raid on your locality was not easily forgotten!

In the case of a successful enemy incursion by sea, the blanket of censorship would have been wrapped even tighter around the ability to report it. Revealing it would have been unthinkable. The need to safeguard security and preserve civilian morale would always hold sway.

However, as it turned out, it *was* worth making that search of the island's wartime press, principally because it shed some light on the facts behind what had seemed a possible, albeit particularly disturbing, lead on the identities of British personnel allegedly killed in the raid. The rumours of British casualties, victims of the firefight, were certainly not uncommon on the Isle of Wight after the war. Precisely who they were had never been suggested but, hardly surprisingly and in line with the German naval officer's story outlined to Gareth Sprack in France, the consensus among the story-tellers was that the victims must have been in the military – most likely soldiers on guard duty at the radar site. If so, might they have been buried on the island? Could particulars of their deaths be found in contemporary, or later, records?

Despite the strong probability of an official cover-up obscuring, or perhaps entirely eliminating, background detail such as this, it obviously made sense to cast the researcher's net over this aspect of the tale. A good place to start was likely to be Ventnor Cemetery, the closest major graveyard to St Lawrence. Specifically, a look at the records for those buried there during the 1939–45 conflict in an official war grave might reveal something of note. At the top of the alphabetical list compiled for such burials at Ventnor by the Commonwealth War Graves Commission was an intriguing entry – a member of the British armed forces who died in August 1943. In fact, the precise date of death was recorded as the 17th, the day after the most likely date for the German raid. It came as something of a surprise to discover that the grave was that of a young woman – 23-year-old Dorothy Maud Arnold, a private in the Auxiliary Territorial Service (ATS), the women's section of the British Army throughout the war.

Dorothy who is named among the official ATS list of its wartime casualties, was a local girl from Steephill Down Road, Upper Ventnor. The cemetery, a matter of yards from her family home, was therefore an unsurprising place to find her grave. But how had she died? There were certainly female operatives at RAF St Lawrence, but they were members of the Women's Auxiliary Air Force (WAAF). While some ATS women were employed at radar stations operated by the army, it would have been unusual for one to be employed at a RAF site. Perhaps Dorothy had inadvertently been caught up in the crossfire while carrying out some other task as part of her army duties. Maybe she had just happened to be in the wrong place at the wrong time. However, from a copy of her death certificate emerged a wholly different story. Dorothy had apparently died of natural causes – pulmonary tuberculosis. Intriguingly, her occupation at the time of death was recorded on the certificate as shop assistant. There was no reference to her military service with the ATS, despite her burial in a war grave, and her place of death was noted as being the family home in Ventnor.

Was this part of a conspiracy to mask the truth about the circumstances of her death? It was tempting to consider this as a possibility. Dorothy was interred under her army rank and service number (W/54161), so why had the official record of her death described her as a civilian shop worker? Or, to put it another way, why would a civilian shop worker qualify for burial in a war grave? On the face of it, this did seem to present something of an anomaly. The rules governing burial in a war grave, however, are rather more complex than they might at first appear. Could the Commonwealth War Graves Commission provide an answer to the puzzle?

When contacted, the CWGC pointed out:

'The information that we hold within our records was provided to us by the service authorities during and following the end of the war. They would have informed us, as the Imperial War Graves Commission, that Private Arnold was serving with the Auxiliary Territorial Service (ATS) at the time of her death and that we should therefore commemorate her as a war casualty ... Since the ATS was a female branch of the British Army ... the Commission would commemorate them regardless of the cause of death as long as they were still serving. It therefore did not matter where she died or how but that she was in service at the time of her death. Since the service authorities declared that we should commemorate her, this should explain why she is commemorated by the Commission in perpetuity.'

So the anomaly remained. According to her death certificate, Dorothy was *not* serving in the ATS at the time of her death. She was working in a shop. A further study of the qualification criteria for war graves, however, identified a second category of entitlement. Personnel who had been discharged or retired from the military before their death as a result of injury or illness would also qualify for a war grave if it could be proven that the injury or illness which had led to their death had been either directly caused or exacerbated by their wartime military service.

Pulmonary tuberculosis (TB) is a contagious bacterial infection affecting the lungs which may spread to other organs. It would seem that Dorothy's service with the ATS was judged to have significantly contributed to the fatal consequences of her illness. Her death was announced in both the Newport-based *Isle of Wight County Press,* which circulated, as it does today, throughout the island, and the Ventnor area's own newspaper, the *Isle of Wight Mercury*.

The latter carried a short news report in its edition of Friday, 20 August:

'We hear with deep regret of the death on Tuesday evening of Miss Dorothy Maud Arnold, daughter of Mr and Mrs C. Arnold, of Steephill Down Road. Miss Arnold, who was 23 years of age, had served in the ATS until ill health brought about her discharge. Subsequently, she was for a time, up to a few months ago, employed as an assistant at the local Co-operative store. Her father [Charles] is an employee of the Ventnor [Urban District] Council and, with his wife and other members of his family, will be assured of the deep sympathy of all who know them.'

Thus it seems safe to rule out this unfortunate young woman's untimely death from any link to an attempt to cover up all traces of a German landing on the Isle of Wight coast. This particular trawl of archived local newspapers had succeeded in catching the proverbial red herring.

Also buried at Ventnor's cemetery, in the only other war grave there from 1943, is Royal Artillery gunner, 40-year-old Richard Wood, who was serving on the mainland with 202 Fixed Defence Regiment at the time of his 22 February death. Ventnor was Gunner Wood's home town.

The solitary 1939–45 war grave in St Lawrence churchyard also dates from 1943. It is that of Flight Lieutenant Jack Bartrum, a 25-year-old pilot with the RAF Volunteer Reserve attached to the highly secretive No. 161 (Special Duties) Squadron. This was one of three RAF squadrons whose job was to carry out missions with the Special Operations Executive (SOE), tasked primarily with the dropping and collection of secret agents and equipment into and from Nazi-occupied Europe. Jack Bartrum died on 16 May 1943 while on operational duty. His war burial at St Lawrence is explained by the fact that the family's home was in the village.

Also in the south of the island, at St Andrew's Churchyard in Chale village, the only World War Two war grave is that of 49-year-old Home Guardsman J.E.B. Cheverton, a local man who died in February 1944. At Niton's St John the Baptist Churchyard there is also just one war grave from the 1939–45 conflict. Diana Biddlecombe, a 33-year-old Wren serving on the mainland at HMS *Daedalus*, Lee-on-Solent, died in October 1944. Unlike the previous two locations, St Boniface's Churchyard in Bonchurch does have a war grave from 1943, that of Sergeant John Price, a navigator and wireless operator with the RAF Volunteer Reserve at the time of his death on 10 February when he was attached to No. 141 Squadron, then engaged on long-range intruder missions over occupied Europe. It seems he had local connections with the village.

Recalling the former (1798–1960) Parkhurst (later Albany) Barracks, the Isle of Wight's military cemetery at Parkhurst, just north of Newport, contains the graves of several armed forces casualties of the Second World War, but only five whose deaths occurred in 1943. None of these men lost their lives in August. However, for two reasons, it was worth examining the known details for all five fatalities. Perhaps they had died later in the year of injuries sustained in an August raid, although, as it turned out, this could only be considered in the context of one man's death; the others all occurred in the first half of the year. The second scenario, of course, was that nagging possibility that an enemy landing had taken place on a different date to that supported by the majority of the evidence which had come to light.

In chronological order, the first two deaths occurred on 4 February. Both fatalities were Royal Marines serving with No. 41 (RM) Commando. Marines James Dawson, aged twenty, from Aberdeenshire, and 23-year-old Charles Jude, from Berwickshire, were victims of a tip and run raid inflicted by a quartet of Fw-190 fighter-bombers on the town of Ryde which claimed the lives of eleven people, including four servicemen, and injured sixty-two others. Much of 41 Commando's early training during the winter of 1942–43 was carried out on the Isle of Wight, with a force of 400-plus men billeted in the homes of residents and some larger buildings at Ryde and several of its neighbouring villages in the island's north-eastern district.

Marine Harry Guinan, aged twenty-three, from Essex, died on 24 April. He trained on the Isle of Wight with No. 40 (RM) Commando, who were billeted at Sandown, Shanklin and Ventnor in the build-up to Operation Jubilee, the ill-fated August 1942 raid on Dieppe, and died later of his wounds.

Eire-born Frederick Maitland Eagar, aged forty-seven, with family links to Shrewsbury, is by some distance the highest-ranking 1943 war casualty buried at Parkhurst. A lieutenant-colonel in the King's Shropshire Light Infantry at the time of his death on 30 June, his island burial is a curious case. Probate records from January 1944 record his most recent home address as Llandudno in north Wales and his place of death as London. To add to the puzzle, none of the KSLI's battalions, regular or territorial, featured among the succession of light infantry formations which carried out home defence duties at various periods of the war on the Isle of Wight.

So why was Colonel Eagar buried at Parkhurst Cemetery? What was his Isle of Wight link in 1943? And how had he died? Despite his status, there were surprisingly few leads to follow up from the numerous sources which now exist to provide details of ancestry and the wartime records of service personnel. The answers to all three of those key questions remained strangely elusive. Unlikely though a connection between Eagar and a rumoured German raid appeared, things were not adding up in the case of the King's Shropshire Light Infantry officer.

The obvious solution to this particular puzzle was to secure a copy of the officer's death certificate. It soon became clear that his death was registered on the Isle of Wight in 1943, not in London. He had died in Newport borough, just up the road to Cowes at Parkhurst itself, making the military cemetery an obvious location for his burial. The precise place of death was certainly interesting. Colonel Eagar had died in the deputy governor's house at Parkhurst's famous prison, where he was a guest. The formal cause of death was noted as 'from natural causes, namely coronary thrombosis'. A post-mortem examination and organ analysis had been ordered. Whatever the officer was doing on the island in the summer of 1943, and it remains unclear, he had died suddenly from a heart attack.

The last of Parkhurst's five 1943 war burials was that of Flight Sergeant Arthur Cox, aged twenty-three, who had enlisted in the RAF Volunteer Reserve but at the time of his death on 5 October was serving with No. 434 (RCAF) Squadron, one of several non-Canadians who flew with the bomber squadron following its formation in the UK, at RAF Tholthorpe, North Yorkshire, on 13 June 1943, three months before its first operational sortie, a bombing raid across the Alps to Milan, Italy. The young airman was therefore an early casualty for the fledgling unit. Precisely how he met his death is unclear, but it was not uncommon for the bodies of air crew to be washed ashore on the Isle of Wight during the war and it is difficult to imagine how Arthur, whose family were from Surrey, could have been involved with a seaborne enemy raid on an Isle of Wight radar station, despite the obvious fact that the station was also run by the RAF.

There is one other war grave at Parkhurst worthy of investigation. Located at the cemetery's plot eleven, grave 148 contains the remains of an unidentified British soldier, a casualty of the Second World War. It is certainly unusual to have no identifying details for a wartime serviceman interred on home soil. Could *this* burial be linked to the legendary German raid? Was the soldier's ID, his army unit and his date of death deliberately withheld by high authority for fear of providing an undesired clue to an incident the British Government was anxious to keep secret for an indefinite period after the war?

When contacted about the mystery burial, the Commonwealth War Graves Commission provided a response which, in the context of 'raid on the radar' research, was something of a let-down:

'The only information we hold in our archive relating to the casualty was provided by a garrison engineer on the Isle of Wight in 1942, who wrote that cemetery records showed a burial of an unidentified soldier had taken place on 4 July 1940, name unknown, found drowned.'

Clearly, if the soldier died in 1940, his passing can have no relationship to a 1943 raid.

If the search is extended beyond the Ventnor area's cemeteries and graveyards, and the central Parkhurst military cemetery, it is possible to find war graves from 1943 elsewhere in the island.

The civic cemetery at Shanklin contains the burial sites of four service personnel who died in that year. Private Walter Dimond, aged twenty-eight and serving with the territorials of the Hampshire Regiment's 7th Battalion, was a local man whose death at the end of March cannot be linked to the suggested dates for the German landing. Royal Naval Petty Officer Alfred Hunt thirty-five-years of age, another Shanklin man, was serving with the naval shore base at HMS *Dundonald* in Ayrshire when he died at the end of May, his detachment from the island an obvious reason for discounting him from the equation. Royal Marine William Morris, fifty, is buried at Shanklin because of his family links to nearby Ventnor and not through any military action on the island. The same can be said for Petty Officer Albert Spencer, from Shanklin, the eldest at fifty-seven, who died in July.

Royal Artillery gunner, James Searson, forty-nine years old, occupies the solitary war grave from 1943 in neighbouring Sandown Cemetery. Serving with 527 (Hampshire) Coast Regiment, a territorial unit, on the Isle of Wight when he died in April, his burial at Sandown is unsurprising owing to his local residency and while the circumstances of his death are not clear, the date in April would seem to preclude any link with the rumoured German landing. There are nineteen war graves in the graveyard at Sandown's Christ Church but just two are occupied by casualties from the Second World War, and neither of these relate to a death in 1943.

Further afield, Ryde Borough Cemetery is the last resting place for two servicemen whose deaths occurred in 1943. Both 33-year-old Henry Willett, a Royal Engineers sapper who died in February, and Wilfred Hart, twenty-two, a chief motor mechanic with the Royal Navy who lost his life in November, owe the location of their graves in Ryde to local status rather than involvement with a local incident. Not far from Ryde, five of the eight war burials in St Helens Churchyard date from the 1939–45 conflict but none from 1943. At Newport's civic cemetery there are just four graves of servicemen who died during World War Two and none of these men are recorded as burials from 1943. It is a similar story in other parts of the island.

A substantial number of civilians, casualties of enemy action, are also buried in war graves at various sites on the island. While the remains of several who died in 1943 occupy graves in the Ventnor area, including the three St Catherine's Light keepers, none of these deaths can readily be attributed to a seaborne enemy assault in mid–August or earlier in the summer. In summary, if any British casualties from the apparently hushed-up German raid were interred on the Isle of Wight instead of being sent home – assuming they were from the mainland in the first place – the whereabouts of their final resting places are anything but obvious.

Before leaving the vexed question of possible raid casualties, there is another curious story which might possibly be related to the fabled 1943 landing at St Lawrence's radar station. The story comes from Dr David Tomalin, the Isle of Wight's retired county archaeologist. Some years ago, while he was still heading up the archaeology service, he received a telephone call from George Haynes in Bonchurch, the ancient village which lies to the east of Ventnor.

'He said he had a collection of flints and suggested we ought to see it. Eventually I did go to see him myself at his home near the village lake and found that he did indeed have a wonderful collection of flint implements. He told me he had found the flints in fields in which he had worked during the war.'

The flints were of course fascinating but Dr Tomalin's attention was then diverted to something else in Mr Haynes' possession.

'He said he had written a book and suggested the county might like to publish it. He had typed it all out and I got the impression the copy he showed me was probably the only one there was. I was unsure what to do about it but I took it from him and then, I confess, I "sat on it" for two or three weeks.'

When the book was eventually shown to them, the island's education service, enchanted by its content, were soon discussing having 100 copies made for distribution among local schools. This led to its publication by the Isle of Wight Teachers' Centre in 1984. Added Dr Tomalin:

'The book was entitled *It used to be like this* and it was basically Mr Haynes' reminiscences about the Undercliff [the coastal tract, which includes St Lawrence, west of Ventnor]. One of the chapters was called *The dead German* in which he described finding a body one morning on the beach near St Lawrence during the war. It was that of a young boy, aged about seventeen, of typical German appearance, with blonde hair and blue eyes which were staring out at the sky. He was dressed in naval uniform. With help, Mr Haynes put the body into a wheelbarrow and wheeled it to his potting shed. Despite notifying the police and the ARP about the body's discovery, nobody came to collect it and two weeks later it was still there! Mr Haynes and those around him were too frightened by then to look inside the shed again. There was great relief when, eventually, the body of the poor young German was taken away.'

Finding the correct context for this quirky, if somewhat unpalatable, tale is difficult. It would not have been that surprising to discover the body of a German naval serviceman on an Isle of Wight beach in wartime. We do not have a date for this particular discovery so any attempt to link it with a 1943 enemy raid is problematic, and the more so because neither of the two accounts from Germany refer to a fatality among the raiding force while they were on the Isle of Wight. The only death suggested among their number was the man who, according to Gareth Sprack's informant, died on the way home. Though it seems improbable, it is still of course possible that his body, either by deliberate or accidental means, ended up in the sea and was later washed ashore on a beach at or near St Lawrence. Who he was and how his body was eventually disposed of after its extended stay in the Haynes potting shed remains a mystery.

Was it examined for a formal declaration of death by a local doctor? If so there would have been a written record made of this, as there would of any post-mortem examination carried out. The cause of death would have been noted and, assuming the young man was still in possession of his ID tag when found by George Haynes, so would a clue to his identity. This would also, of course, have applied to any British casualties of the raid. No medical records which can directly be linked to a mid-war German landing appear to have survived on the Isle of Wight but there is an indication that something of the sort may have surfaced, albeit temporarily it would seem, some years after the war before being re-submerged by official decree.

Again, this intriguing episode in the 'raid on the radar' tale comes from Gareth Sprack, who told me:

'I give quite a few talks on the island and occasionally I will throw in the story of the German raid as a fishing exercise, just to see if anything comes back. On one occasion, and I don't recall now when or where it was, I did exactly that. I didn't make too much of it but at the end of the talk a guy came up and told me he had something to say which he thought might interest me. As I remember it, he said he had a friend who was, or had been, a GP in Ventnor and who had taken over the practice in the early Fifties on the retirement of the doctor who had been there during the war. It seems that, on reading through his predecessor's paperwork, he turned up something that grabbed his attention, something to do with the German landing. He was apparently so intrigued by what he had read that he went to great lengths to find out more about it. I think he may have put something in the *Isle of Wight County Press.* Certainly, the impression I was given was that he announced his finding publicly in some way.

'Nothing much had seemed to come of this so when the guy telling me the story bumped into the doctor about six months later, he asked him, "What's become of that business about the German raid?" He may have worded it slightly differently but that was the gist of it. His doctor friend's reply was brief – and surprising. "I don't want to know about that – don't ask me about it," he said, giving the clear impression that he had been visited by someone in authority who had warned him against saying anything further. If there had been British soldiers killed in the raid, I suppose there must have been something to do with this in the medical notes he had come across and, obviously, this would have been bound to raise his interest.'

The precise origins of this story are hard to pin down, especially as there is only the vaguest of time periods – the early 1950s – to go on. Following a search of Kelly's Directories for the town and its neighbourhood in both 1937–38 and 1951, either side of the war years, prominent Ventnor historian Michael Freeman has suggested Dr J.B. Williamson as a likely identity for the town's wartime doctor apparently involved in the medical examination of raid casualties. 'It appears Dr Williamson was the medical officer for the area during the period and probably the leading physician. His practice was at Southcliff on Belgrave Road,' said Michael. As to his possible successor, Michael, a key member of Ventnor & District Local History Society, pointed out that the 1951 Kelly's edition 'has quite a few doctors listed for Ventnor, one of whom was Prausnitz'. The quest to flesh out the bones of Gareth Sprack's story of the Ventnor doctors is continuing, but Michael Freeman's reference to Dr Prausnitz, one of the town's most renowned former medical practitioners, is certainly worth examining further.

Professor Carl Prausnitz is remembered in medical circles the world over for making a fundamental contribution to the study and development of immunology and has been called 'the father of clinical allergy,' having made the crucial observation in 1921 that the blood of an allergic individual contained a transferable factor, subsequently shown to be an antibody.[5] However, in the context of researching possible links to the 1943 German raid, it is *his* bloodline which holds a particular fascination. Prausnitz was born on 11 October 1876 to mixed German-English parentage in Hamburg, Germany's second largest city. In 1935, having left his clinical studies work at the University of Breslau (coincidentally the home town of Alfred Laurence), he arrived on the Isle of Wight, which he had several times before visited when staying with English relatives, to become a general practitioner in the Ventnor area, working from Bonchurch, the home village of his mother's family. He practiced as Dr Prausnitz Giles (adding his mother's maiden name to his surname) and was a dedicated and popular GP who continued to serve the local community for nearly thirty years until his death in 1963.

So Prausnitz was in Ventnor before, during and after the Second World War. Indeed, he held a highly unusual distinction through serving as a captain in the town's Home Guard while in possession of the Iron Cross 1st Class, awarded to him in Germany during the First World War when he served, as hygiene advisor to an army corps on active service in Belgium and France.

Given his background, might it be the case that, in the decade following the war, it was Prausnitz who came across the medical notes made by a recently retired doctor which, according to Gareth Sprack's story, apparently related to victims of the German wartime raid and led to the ultimately aborted search for further information. Dr Prausnitz was not, of course, a new doctor in town in the early Fifties, but he could have acquired new patients, and their medical histories, from a former colleague. It does not seem difficult to make the case that Prausnitz might well have had more motivation than most in Ventnor to pursue the matter.

If the story of George Haynes' discovery of a young German's body is something of a hard fit with the two detailed accounts of the St Lawrence attack, it is more than matched in that awkward regard by another of the many local 'raid tales' involving dead enemy servicemen. In 2014, having read my renewed online appeal for information from Isle of Wight residents about the landing, Stuart Hersey, range warden at the RFCA's (Reserve Forces & Cadets Association's) Newtown Ranges in the island's northwest, emailed me with a fascinating item:

'The gist of it is that a serving [wartime] soldier from Shanklin, home on leave at the time of the raid, was knocked up at home and put on a truck with a mixed bag of military personnel. They were driven to the site of the landing and were ordered to recover bodies, equipment and all traces of the enemy from the beach. I was told by the soldier's son that the bodies were taken to Parkhurst Forest for burial. All the personnel involved were threatened with severe punishments if any souvenirs were taken or they spoke about the German raid to anyone at all.'

The implication here is clearly that there were a large number of dead Germans on the shore, nudging the story closer to the 'bodies on the beach' category of multifarious legends described in chapter 1. Stuart Hersey reinforced that view when I spoke with him later.

'I think he [the soldier's son] said his father had spoken of *burnt* German bodies and had told his son that he was away from home for a couple of days. When asked about it further he said he had "helped to clear something up" but he was unable to say any more, though he did tell his son that, if they were asked by anyone who felt something suspicious was going on, they were to say that it was a British commando exercise using soldiers dressed as Germans. Highly risky, I would have thought! As a regular soldier he would obviously have been in serious trouble if he had spoken about what had really happened – if anything happened at all.'

And that, of course, is the point. This is pretty much a typical 'flaming seas' tale. No doubt it has been faithfully handed down but the truth behind it may not have been apparent even to the soldiers involved, masked by a mist of propaganda. But there is one major difference. Not only is this particular story divorced from the 1940 setting occupied by most similar tales, it seems to have been linked firmly to the German raid of 1943, a possible mix of fantasy and fact.

If we continue to place the emphasis on 15–16 August 1943 as the most probable date for a German landing, pinpointing the identity of the army unit most likely to have been on guard duty at RAF St Lawrence that night has proved as frustratingly difficult as trying to identify the names of any individual casualties. As noted, responsibility for beach defence duties on the Isle of Wight had passed in June 1943 from the 214th Independent Infantry Brigade (Home) to a sub-district of the 47th (London) Infantry Division. The latter had been formed as part of the Territorial Army in November 1940 by re-designation of the 2nd London Division and by 1942 it was under the command of Major General Alfred Robinson of the Green Howards.[6]

The 47th Division's overall order of battle included units from the 4th, 5th and 6th London Infantry Brigades, the 25th Infantry Brigade and a number of divisional troops. It remained in the UK on home defence and related activity throughout the war. Elements of the 47th Division were sent to the island at different times to form the sub-district and it is clear that defence of the isle's southern sector, including the RAF radar stations regularly changed hands. In mid-August 1943 there appears to have been a single infantry brigade and one field (artillery) regiment, plus the island's Home Guardsmen, in place to defend the shores of Wight.

However, few accessible war diaries covering the relevant August period appear to have survived and those records that do refer to Isle of Wight defence – for example, from a Royal Corps of Signals divisional detachment – provide no clue to a seaborne incursion by the enemy, nor indeed to the composition and numerical strength of the troops and Royal Artillery gunners in place to defend St Lawrence radar station. A relatively small number is likely.

It is known that, at least initially, the station was guarded by a detachment of men from the RAF Regiment, which had been formed with the express purpose of defending air force sites, but confirmation is lacking on whether or not this was still the case in the summer of 1943. Though precise timings are unclear, it appears, too, that at some stage men from the Royal Military Police Vulnerable Points Wing (the 'Blue Hats'), set up in 1941 to patrol and guard key installations and infrastructure, were assigned to protect the radar station, as they were at other sensitive sites elsewhere on the Isle of Wight. This may have happened as a result of the raid.

As for the defensive armament at the station, the initial provision was just two Browning machine guns. Anti-aircraft protection was provided from St Boniface Down although records indicate that the nearest *heavy* anti-aircraft gun site to St Lawrence in the summer of 1943 was eleven miles to the northwest on the Back of the Wight coast at Grange Farm, Brighstone, one of ten heavy AA sites listed as being operational on the island in June under the command of 35th Anti-Aircraft Brigade. Brighstone's windswept gun site was well equipped with four 3.7-inch guns, two fixed and two mobile, together with a Bofors light AA weapon. It is believed that further heavy AA sites were later added west of Brighstone and at Blackgang Chine and St Catherine's Point, both much closer to St Lawrence's radar station. Those three additional sites were certainly active during the war – a reaction to an enemy raid?[7]

If we are to look for possible further consequences of a German landing, a comprehensive insight into the overall defence strategy for the island as a whole, as revised by the 47th Division sub-district in the period after the rumoured seaborne attack, has fortunately survived. In 1987 an extensive collection of documents from the files of the 20th (East Wight – Nunwell) Battalion of the Hampshire Home Guard was placed in the care of the island's Record Office.[8] Headquartered at historic Nunwell House, near Brading, hence its elongated title, it was commanded initially by the house's owner, Brigadier General Cecil Aspinall-Oglander, then in his sixties,[9] later succeeded by Lieutenant Colonel C.W. Brannon. This was one of two HG battalions on the island, along with the 19th which covered the West Wight.

The preserved records, four box-loads, are actually those of the 20th Battalion's B Company, which operated in the Sandown area while A Company had responsibility for the Ryde district, C Company covered the environs of Shanklin and D Company operated in the area farthest south around Ventnor. Many of the boxed documents, however, apply to the East Wight Battalion as a whole, and in some cases to the two-battalion Home Guard in its entirety.

Among the most significant of these is a set of key instructions which must have been issued to both HG battalions from 47th Division's sub-district HQ in Newport. Marked 'secret,' this document is dated 28 August 1943 but had been 'signed off' on the 25th – just ten days after what appears the most likely date for the St Lawrence landing. Potentially therefore, it is highly significant evidence.

Interestingly, the instruction sets out plans to augment 'until further notice' regular troops with Home Guard 'as soon as possible in emergency' at a number of vulnerable coastal locations in the south of the island. These areas specifically include Niton, St Lawrence and Ventnor as well as Shanklin and Sandown further up the south-eastern shoreline. From this we can deduce two things. First, beach security in the southern sector was to be reinforced. Second, if we accept that the Germans *had* raided the radar station at St Lawrence a matter of days earlier, it would seem the Home Guard had not been called out to defend it on that occasion.

The same instruction also directs the Home Guard to relieve as soon as possible regular troops at Freshwater, in the island's far west. This statement is ambiguous – did it mean the Home Guard would generally be taking over defensive responsibility from garrison troops or would they be expected to provide relief only in the event of an emergency, which certainly would include a landing by an enemy force anywhere in the vicinity of the Back of the Wight coast.

Presumably, this would have been clarified for all concerned. Whatever the precise meaning, it seems clear that the military defence of the lengthy stretch of coastline between the southern and western tips of the Isle of Wight was about to undergo a significant overhaul – as would be expected had the enemy successfully mounted a surprise raid just over a week earlier.

Another document in the boxed collection, dated 25 September, alerts Home Guard units active in the Isle of Wight to a revised defence scheme for the island as a whole, replacing a predecessor scheme drawn up in July 1942. It is prefaced by excerpts from a speech made by Winston Churchill during a rallying broadcast the previous May in which the PM had stressed that the importance of Britain's Home Guard had increased rather than diminished. The revised plan covers a wide breadth of detail about defensive measures about to come into force.

A fascinating feature is a risk assessment of potential German attacks. The form of attack considered the most likely was an airborne assault. A full-scale invasion or major raid was rated as 'possible but at present considered unlikely' while a CW (chemical weapon – meaning gas) assault was thought to be 'always possible'. If there had already been an enemy attack by sea a month or so earlier (though the island's military command would not have risked referring to this in a circulated document, even one marked 'secret' as was the case here) would this have been regarded as a 'major raid'? It is an arguable point and because of this it is difficult to be certain about the level of concern among the military authorities in Newport over the possibility of another raid of similar size along the same stretch of coastline, or any other part of the island's coast. Certainly, they couldn't afford to take any chances.

The island military force's overall intention was clearly spelt out in the re-drawn defence scheme. It is inconceivable that it would have changed from that defined in the plan it replaced. Put simply, it was 'to destroy the invaders'. The overarching role of the field force troops of 47th Division's sub-district operating in a sector under attack was put in similarly simple terms: 'to counter-attack' in a concerted attempt to bring about the desired destruction of the enemy – something those in the southern sector appear not to have successfully achieved in August. The Home Guard's role was set out in detail under an evocative heading which is especially pertinent in the context of the present work: 'In the event of a commando raid ...'

Their job was explained as (a) local defence; (b) locating, harrying and delaying the enemy; (c) passing on information; and (d) preventing a get-away by sea. No Home Guard position would be regarded as 'rigid and unchangeable ... and Home Guard units and sub-units at all times must be ready on receipt of orders to take immediate action against enemy troops landing within five miles.' Meanwhile, Royal Artillery units were tasked with moving to points from where they could bring fire to bear on eight listed 'get-away' beaches. Four of these were in the northeast of the island in the Bembridge area (at Bembridge Point, Tyne Hall, Foreland and Whitecliff Bay). In the southeast, Luccombe Chine was also listed. The remaining three were all in the St Lawrence area – at Steephill Bay, Battery Bay/Puckaster Cove and immediately below the radar station itself at Woody Bay. The nearby rail tunnel on the branch line from Merstone would be blocked (as would Ventnor tunnel, on the principal rail line from Ryde, and Sandown, further up the main line) by the Southern Railway's own Home Guard.

Nothing among the archived records indicates whether the isle's revised defence scheme included use of the Home Guard's Auxiliary Units, the shadowy 'stay behind' force secretly tasked since 1940, in the event of a full-scale invasion of the Wight, with resisting the enemy as far as possible while just about everyone else was evacuated to the mainland. But the units' total omission from the boxed 1943 documents is no surprise – the very existence of the Auxiliaries would remain a secret for decades to come. What *is* clear from the preserved papers is that St Lawrence, so recently the target for attack if we accept the night of 15–16 August as the probable date of the German commando raid, was now a target for defence.

Chapter 9

Analysis: The Case for Consideration

T he point has been made in this book that stories of wartime German landings in the United Kingdom need to be evaluated with a high degree of scepticism. The proffered details may seem compellingly genuine; the story-tellers too. Indeed, the tales are mostly put forward by people who have an absolute and unshakable belief that they are telling the truth – and it is time the government did likewise and finally admit that an enemy force *did* set foot in Britain on active military service during the Second World War. Summarily dismissing the stories as myths without taking a proper look at the apparent facts which underpin them is unfair to their purveyors and yet, when the facts *are* properly investigated, the status of a myth is almost always confirmed. So what makes this account of the fabled German landing in the Isle of Wight any different? Why should the reader set the 'raid on the radar' tale apart from all the others?

The Isle of Wight story is supported by years of local rumour and speculation passed down through the post-war generations. The rumours have been so persistent and so strongly repeated that many islanders, especially those in the Ventnor area, had long accepted the seaborne raid as an inarguable truth. But then, virtually all of the German landing legends can point to this. The story described in this book comes with the benefit of first-hand local evidence from people who were there at the time. Some of this has been very useful in corroborating details from other sources. Yet, in line with the catalogue of similar tales from the mainland, it is almost certainly the case that there is nobody alive today who can say, 'Yes, I saw Germans land on the Isle of Wight in the 1939-45 war'.

What sets this story apart from all the others is threefold. First, the key distinguishing factor of not being set in the 'invasion scare' summer of 1940, as so many accounts are, and not suggesting an invasion – foiled or otherwise – at all. The island story is firmly enshrined in the mid-war period and tells of a far more believable commando-style raid with specific purposes entirely understandable from the enemy's perspective. There is no need to stretch the imagination to any great extent to see how this could have happened and why the German raiding force was assembled in the way that it seems it was. In other words, the story makes sense.

The second distinguishing factor is that, despite the apparent governmental cover-up, some official written evidence appears to have avoided the censor's airbrush. Admittedly, the ARP record does not categorically confirm a German landing at St Lawrence in 1943 – the obvious assumption being that the compilers of the diary were ordered to say or write nothing more – but it does come tantalisingly close to doing so with its very specific mention of 'dinghies full of Germans off the Ventnor coast'. Other non-verbal testimony, such as the documents relating to the revised defence scheme for the island drawn up within days of the probable date of the raid, also contribute significantly to a wealth of unchallengeable written evidence which has no equal in any of the other legendary accounts of hushed-up enemy landings in wartime.

But it is the third distinguishing factor which really elevates the 'raid on the radar' legend onto a level far and above that on which those other stories awkwardly sit. There is evidence, very compelling evidence, from Germany testifying to the authenticity of the St Lawrence raid.

It is surely incontestable that the two quite separate German accounts of the raid, provided by men who said they took part in it, are truthful accounts. Some of the details may differ – the most glaring being the issue of whether British soldiers were taken prisoner or killed in the firefight – but essentially the two accounts are variants of the same story. The questions must be asked: why would these men lie; what would be the point of that? We have no reason to question their motives for telling their stories. We have no reason – and this is especially true of Dietrich Andernacht, a highly respected and learned historian himself – to doubt their integrity.

The lack of official German records to confirm the raid will be seen by many as a surprising omission – as will the fact that nothing has emerged post-war in that country to verify the authenticity of the story. From the German perspective, this was an operation worthy of admiration, a matter of some pride. Why have the Germans apparently made nothing of this, either during the war itself or in the decades since? Possible reasons for this have been suggested in this work, the most probable being that the British succeeded a long time ago in discovering and then quickly eliminating the former wartime enemy's documented references to it.

Today, the *Bundesarchiv*, Germany's national archival service, appears to have no knowledge of a raid. Mirroring conjecture in the UK, its best bet, when contacted, was that the landing might have been carried out by the *Brandenburgers*, Nazi Germany's special forces units during the war. On the face of it, this appeared to be a perfectly reasonable suggestion. The *Brandenburgers*, composed mainly of Slavic personnel, operated in almost all theatres of the European war. Units took part in the invasions of Poland, Denmark and Norway; in the Battle of France; in Operation Barbarossa against the USSR; in Finland and Greece; and in the invasions of Crete, Romania, Bulgaria and Yugoslavia. Yet, despite an extended archival quest which is continuing in Germany, nothing has so far emerged in the search for evidence to reinforce the view that they were involved in a raid on the Isle of Wight.

The far more likely scenario is the one described by Alfred Laurence – that RAF St Lawrence was raided in 1943 by a seaborne enemy force composed primarily of an army convalescent unit (with naval support), men in the final stages of preparedness for their return to the front line.

The reason for high-level secrecy in Britain about the raid at the time it happened is entirely understandable. The point has been made earlier in the book that an event such as this *had* to be hushed-up by high authority The panic and negative effect on public morale which would have followed disclosure of an incident such as this might have proved catastrophic. News of the enemy fighting on the Isle of Wight certainly would not have helped the British war effort.

It is much harder to determine why the 'raid on the radar' remains a secret today, more than seventy years later. Did the official denial become so entrenched in the British psyche that, as the years rolled by, exposure of the 1943 raid would have caused national embarrassment? Gareth Sprack probably hit the proverbial nail on the head when he commented:

'In one respect I can see why the British would keep this secret for so long. We have this thing about Churchill, the great saviour of Britain in World War Two, who has made this proud statement that there was no successful commando raid, or enemy landing of any sort, in the UK during the war. Are we even now ready, effectively, to discredit Churchill even in the smallest of ways?'

The problem for the British authorities has always been that the longer this clearly unsustainable denial continues, the more potentially embarrassing it would become at the time of its eventual exposure as a lie – and the more the reputation of Britain's magnificent war leader might suffer as a result of this. The British nation deserves to learn the truth about the 'raid on the radar'. It is part of our national history. Continued denial serves no justifiable purpose.

In January 2016, as this book was being finalised with the evidence collated, I submitted a request to the Ministry of Defence under the terms of the Freedom of Information Act, as follows:

'Is it still the official position of the Ministry of Defence, and the government as a whole, that during World War Two, as stated by the MoD in 1992, "there is no evidence of any German invasion attempt or even German commando-style raids by sea or air. Indeed, there is no evidence in either the most highly classified contemporary British records, or apparently in the contemporary German records, of an actual attempt by the Germans to land in Britain, apart from the Channel Islands, which were occupied by the Germans after the fall of France" …?

'During extensive research into a rumoured mid-war German raid on an Isle of Wight radar station, evidence which strongly contradicts the above assertion has come to light from highly-reputable German sources – supporting a long-held belief, local records and anecdotal evidence on the island that such an incident did indeed take place in the summer of 1943 and subsequently was erased from the historical record, a situation which apparently prevails to this day.

'The German evidence includes statements attesting to the raid by former servicemen who actually took part in the operation. Thus it would appear to be a fact. If this *is* the case, and notwithstanding the understandable need for an initial 'cover up,' it is surely in the interests of the British public, and in those of historical accuracy and completeness, for official acknowledgement finally to be made of an incident which took place more than seventy years ago.'

The Ministry immediately acknowledged the request and targeted 18 February for a response. The target date came and went; there had been no response. Weeks passed and a request for an update on the situation seemed to fall on deaf ears. Finally, on 9 March, the MoD's Information Rights Team emailed its reply. The essential content, unsigned, came as no real surprise:

'Thank you for your email of 22 January … I am treating your correspondence as a request for information under the Freedom of Information Act 2000 … and would like to apologise for the length of time it has taken to respond. A search for the information has now been completed within the Ministry of Defence and I can confirm that no information in scope of your request is held. Under section 16 (Advice and Assistance), given the age of the information, if it has survived it would be held at the National Archives at Kew. Some information on World War Two operations is available in the Official Histories of the participating countries, copies of which may be available in your local lending library. You could also search the official records in the National Army Museum and the Imperial War Museum.'

The remainder of the Ministry's response was generalised information and formal advice relating to the further action available to anyone applying for information under the terms of the Act.

Essentially, then, the position of the Ministry of Defence remains unchanged. A search has been made and nothing has emerged at the Ministry to substantiate the story of the German raid. To suggest this response is in any way disingenuous would be unfair. It is perfectly possible – some might say likely – that the Ministry would not hold any records pertaining to the raid. The suggestion that anything of relevance might be preserved, and therefore publically available, at the National Archives, National Army Museum or Imperial War Museum takes us nowhere. None of these obvious custodians of wartime records appear to have any documentation which might relate to an enemy landing in the Isle of Wight. The only available 'official' information recorded in writing which supports the probability of the raid is that contained at the Isle of Wight Record Office and described within this book.

Whether it was for understandable reasons of preserving the reputation and achievements of Churchill and the nation he so magnificently led to victory in 1945, or merely to brush aside as an irrelevance an incident which did not affect the outcome of the war, or maybe because, having kept quiet about it at the time, its denial has become entrenched in the psyche of the State's hierarchy, the 'raid on the radar' has been erased from our official history and that of the Second World War. Indeed, it was never there in the first place, not because the raid didn't happen but because of a perceived need that it should never be acknowledged publically.

If national records exist at all, their location is probably elsewhere. However, it is of course possible that nothing has been allowed to survive. The airbrush may have eliminated it for good.

Notes

Chapter 1

1. Brechin-born radar pioneer Robert Watson-Watt (1882–1973) left Bewdsey Manor in July 1938 when he was appointed Director of Communications Development, becoming Scientific Advisor on Telecommunications to the Ministry of Aircraft Production the following year. For his outstanding service to his country, Watson-Watt was knighted in 1942. Ten years later his work was further recognised in the form of a £50,000 government award.

2. The last of Bawdsey Manor's four 350-foot steel masts was demolished in 2000 and the manor now houses an international school. Bawdsey additionally acquired a Chain Home Low (CHL) radar facility, one of many established around the British coastline during the war. The post-war history of Orford Ness included its use for a key Atomic Weapons Research Establishment (AWRE) facility, operational between 1956 and 1972.

3. See also *Myths & Legends of the Second World War* by James Hayward, published by The History Press, Stroud, Glos., 2009.

4. The title of Peter Haining's book recalls Jack Higgins' best-selling novel, *The Eagle has Landed,* first published in 1975 and later made into a film, in which the writer imagines a commando-style German landing in eastern England with the audacious aim of kidnapping Winston Churchill. It was re-issued by Penguin, London, in 2013. Peter Haining died in 2007.

5. Several editions of Churchill's acclaimed history have since been produced in varying formats, including a paperback edition from Penguin Classics in May 2005. The work was largely responsible for the award to Churchill in 1953 of the Nobel Prize for Literature.

6. Born in 1929, Australian Phillip Knightley is a journalist, critic, and author, a visiting Professor of Journalism at the University of Lincoln and media commentator on the intelligence services and propaganda. In 2005 he was awarded the Order of Australia for services to journalism and his work as an author.

7. Denis Sefton Delmer died in 1979.

Chapter 2

1. See *Raids in the Late War and their Lessons,* a lecture by Major-General R.E. Laycock published in the journal of the Royal United Service Institute, November 1947, p. 538.

2. Captured in Guernsey on 9 May 1945, Hüffmeier died in 1972, aged 73. See *Death of the Scharnhorst* by John Winton, 1983, reprinted by Cassell Military Paperbacks, 2001.

3. See *The Invasion of France and Germany: 1944–1945 (History of United States Naval Operations in World War II – Vol. 11)* by Samuel Eliot Morison, Castle Books, 2001.

4. See Brendan McNally's 2013 account at www.defensemedianetwork.com/stories/the-geanville-raid.

5. Towed into Saint-Malo harbour the day after her engagement with the German raiding force, submarine-hunter PC-564 was not only successfully salvaged but, following repairs, remained in service with the US Navy until 1963.
6. A month after the assault on Granville, an eighteen-man German sabotage raid was mounted from Jersey against Cap de la Hague in the northwest of the Cotentin. The 5 April mission to destroy installations there failed. The Germans, who landed in rubber boats, were all captured. The end of the war thwarted a further raid planned for 7 May.

Chapter 3
1. The transmitter hut was equipped with a Metropolitan Vickers MB1; the receiver hut with a Cossor RF5.
2. Dunkirk (not be confused with the port of the same name in northern France – spelt Dunkerque in French) is a fairly common place-name in England. In addition to Dunkirk village in Kent, between Faversham and Canterbury, there are small settlements with the same name in several other English counties.
3. As with RAF Ventnor, Boniface Down CD/CHL station survived the immediate post-war streamlining of the coastal radar shield. It was still operational at the start of the 1950s.
4. Some sources suggest the Types 13 and 14 centimetric radars were not introduced to Ventnor until 1944.
5. There would be many other developments at Ventnor's radar station during the remainder of the war and in the post-war years before the RAF ceased operating from the site in 1961. On 6 May 1962 a Douglas C-47A Dakota aircraft, on a scheduled flight from Jersey to Southend via Portsmouth, crashed into the cloud-covered high terrain alongside the radar site, killing twelve of the eighteen occupants (all three crew members and nine passengers). In the same year much of the former RAF compound was taken over by the Civil Aviation Authority which continues to use the site today as a communications station.
6. See also Colin Dobinson's gazetteer of wartime radar sites in *Building Radar: Forging Britain's Early Warning Chain 1939–45,* published by Methurn Ltd., London, 2010.
7. Source: contemporary correspondence with Twining family at Woolverton Manor.
8. At the time of writing (2016) the standby set-house at the former RAF St Lawrence was undergoing conversion to a private house.
9. Later in the war, during the summer of 1943, RAF St Lawrence's conversion for use in a CRDF (cathode ray direction finding) role was under consideration. In the event it was found unsuitable for this but the station nevertheless was employed on a continuous watch for Germany's terror weapons, the V-1 flying bomb and the V-2 rocket, initially between the end of July 1943 and March 1944, and again from 13 June 1944, the day after the first salvo of V-1s was launched against London. RAF St Lawrence was credited with plotting a small number of incoming flying bombs but never detected a V-2. The station's next major use was the plotting of outward Allied aircraft after the June 1944 D-Day invasion. By November 1947 St Lawrence was non-operational, retained on a care and maintenance basis.
10. A second Type 41 radar was installed later at The Needles. Designated M16 in the numbering system, the station's closure followed in September 1945.
11. For a WAAF perspective of life at Bembridge CHL station, see the memoirs of former LACW Betty Chadwick, archived at the RAF Museum in Hendon, London – file ref. X004-2321.

12. Prior to D-Day in 1944, Type 41 centimetric radar was installed in Fort Bembridge and the station which housed it was renumbered as K165. When the European war ended in May 1945 the station was still open – though only on a care and maintenance basis. The original CHL rig had shut down four months earlier.
13. The 1943 TRE memo is filed at the National Archives, with a diagrammatic representation of the watch's target areas, as document AVIA 26/1074.

Chapter 4

1. See new edition of Millar's book, published by Cassell Military Paperbacks, London, 2002.
2. Contemporary papers relating to the training for Operation Biting are among those filed at the National Archives as document AIR 32/8, declassified for public inspection in 1972.
3. The relevant ARP records are held at the Isle of Wight Record Office, Newport, as document IWCC/ARP/L/9 – February-November 1942.
4. Map source: author's collection.
5. Jones was also noted, among a string of wartime achievements, for his joint development with Welsh scientist Joan Curran of 'Window,' strips of metal foil dropped in bundles from aircraft which then appeared on enemy radar screen as 'false bombers.'
6. Admiral Sir William James (1881–1973) acquired his 'Bubbles' nickname after sitting as a child subject for a painting by his grandfather, the Pre-Raphaelite artist John Millais, depicting the five-year-old William gazing enraptured at a bubble he has just blown in the famous advertisement for Pears soap.
7. Browning's comment on Peter Nagel is included in the general's post-raid analysis of training for Operation Biting, preserved at the National Archives among the papers in file AIR 32/8.
8. See AIR 32/8 at National Archives.
9. More than 4,000 Wurzburg radar rigs were eventually produced in various forms.
10. R.V. Jones died in 1987, aged 86.
11. Cook won universal praise for his pivotal role in Operation Biting – and a recall to Australia to command the nation's amphibious training centre at HMAS *Assault* in Port Sapphire, New South Wales. He died, aged 80, in 1985.
12. The Bruneval operation was a notable highlight of General Browning's war. It was not matched later in the conflict when, as deputy commander, he memorably commented during the planning for Operation Market Garden, the doomed 1944 Allied airborne assault in the Netherlands and Germany, 'I think we might be going a bridge too far'. On retirement from the army in 1948, he was appointed Comptroller and Treasurer to the future Queen Elizabeth II, the start of prolonged service with the royal household. Knighted in 1953, he was an Olympic bobsleigh competitor and the husband of author Daphne du Maurier. Browning died in 1965, aged 68.

Chapter 5

1. Conditions at Dachau were to worsen rapidly. Apart from the atrocities committed by guards, the scarce food was continually diminished, the barracks were intolerably overcrowded and the almost complete lack of hygiene resulted in a typhus epidemic which claimed thousands of lives.
2. In Bombay, Lomnitz received news of the death of his former Dachau block-elder, Heinz Eschen, murdered by the SS at the concentration camp on 30 January 1938.

He later compiled a commemorative report – *Heinz Eschen zum Gedenken* – among his reflections of pre-war imprisonment in the Nazi camps.

3. London's Imperial War Museum has a relic of Laurence's war service with the US Army among its Second World War artefacts – a 7.92mm Karabiner 98k weapon, the standard German rifle during the conflict. It seems Laurence found it in a concrete bunker at Equeurdreville, on the outskirts of Cherbourg, in June 1944 and took it home to the States after the war. His widow donated it to the IWM in 1999.

4. The first Dachau trial was the parent case for 123 subsequent proceedings against nearly 500 additional participants in the mass atrocity committed at Dachau. The trial was also the model for the five other main concentration camp tribunals.

5. Mervyn Stockwood, Bishop of Southwark between 1959 and 1980, is arguably best remembered for an appearance with Christian broadcaster Malcolm Muggeridge on the BBC chat show *Friday Night, Saturday Morning* in September 1979, arguing that the film *Monty Python's Life of Brian* was blasphemous. He concluded the discussion by telling John Cleese and Michael Palin that, as in the biblical story of Judas Iscariot, they would 'get [their] thirty pieces of silver.' Stockwood died in 1995, aged 81.

6. Sources: The case of Dr Alfred Laurence, HL Deb. 21 May 1969 vol. 302 cc319-21 / HL Deb. 22 May 1969 vol. 302 cc490-3 –Hansard.

Chapter 6

1. Source: British Library National Life Story Collection: Living memory of the Jewish community – Oskar Winter, interviewed by Milenka Jackson, 1990.

2. Saint Otto of Bamberg (1060–1139) was a German bishop and missionary who is credited with converting much of Pomerania to Christianity. Amdernacht's biography of Otto was supervised by Paul Kirn, professor of medieval history at Frankfurt University.

3. See www.frankfurter-personenlexikon.de.

4. The Institute of City History at the former Carmelite monastery is now recognised as one of Germany's most significant communal archival collections. It also houses, within the monastery's former cloister and refectory, a series of famous murals by Jörg Ratgeb (c. 1480–1426).

5. See particularly *Regesten zur Geschichte der Juden in der Reichsstadt Frankfurt am Main von 1401–1519* by Dietrich Andernacht, published by Hahnsche Buchhandlung, Frankfurt, Germany, 1986.

6. For a comprehensive overview of the *Ersatzhee* see *German Army Order of Battle: The Replacement Army, 1939–45* by W. Victor Madej, published by Game Book Marketing Co., 1984.

7. See *The Island celebrates the end of six years of war with Germany*, article by June Efford in *Island Life* magazine, February / March, 2009.

8. The origin of many of the 'soldier over the cliff' stories is hard to pinpoint. However, in the case of the soldier's girlfriend in Ventnor, the details reproduced here were included in an email from the Lee family who contacted islander Rob Martin in 2009 during his own research into the 'raid on the radar' legend.

9. Following Andrenacht's death his widow, Helga, was able to publish in 2007 a two-volume addendum to her husband's exhaustive study of Frankfurt's Jewish history, covering the story between 1520 and 1616.

Chapter 7

1. The Isle of Wight Rifles were formed to defend the island after the 19th century French invasion scare. The unit served as infantry during the First World War and as coastal

defence artillery during the Second World War. Gareth Sprack's book chronicles the earlier period of the Rifles' story. See *At the Trail: Isle of Wight Rifles 1908–1920*, published by Cross Publishing, Isle of Wight, 2014.

2. After leaving the Isle of Wight, via a brief stay in Cornwall, the 7th SLI moved on 23 June 1943 for training on landing craft in Inverary, Scotland. By August they were in Uckfield, Sussex, later taking part in specific training there. Thereafter they were sent to Hythe, Kent, for further coastal defence tasks.

3. Source: Digital Commons@WOU

4. Convicted of high treason by the British in 1945, William Joyce was hanged in January of the following year.

5. Source: WW2Talk.com – *4th Wilts soldier captured by E-boat crew*, May 2006.

6. What might be termed a hybrid version of the two German accounts features in the autobiography of renowned sports journalist Brian Scovell, who spent his boyhood in the south of the island and heard the 'amazing story' from islander Rob Thornton. 'The incident is said to have come to light some years ago when an islander visiting Germany was confronted with a German war veteran who claimed to have taken part in the landing,' wrote Scovell. See *Thank You Hermann Goering: The Life of a Sports Writer* by Brian Scovell, published by Amberley Publishing, Glos., 2013.

Chapter 8

1. The relevant ARP records are held at the Isle of Wight Record Office, Newport, as document IWCC/ARP/L/11 – February–November 1943.

2. The initials KG were short form for *Kampfgeschwader*, meaning battle squadron or wing, the numbers following denoting the specific Luftwaffe squadron and those before (e.g. 1. and 3.), the *Gruppe* (group) within it.

3. The UK applied Double Summer Time during World War Two by setting the clocks two hours ahead of GMT during the summer and one hour ahead of GMT during the winter.

4. Source: Letter from Philip Davis, November 1973, to Carisbrooke Castle Museum in response to appeal for information for forthcoming exhibition, *The Island at War*, 1974.

5. Source: *Carl Prausnitz; Father of Clinical Allergy*, article by David W. Hide in *Southampton Medical Journal*, vol. 8, no. 2, October 1992.

6. Frequently referred to as the Yorkshire Regiment until the 1920s, the formal title of the Green Howards, a line infantry regiment, was The Green Howards (Alexandra, Princess of Wales's Own Yorkshire Regiment).

7. Sources: (i) *Armageddon. Fed Up With This: A Gunner's Tale* by Derek Nudd, self-published via Matador, Leics., 2015; (ii) *Anti-Aircraft Battery Sites*, review by Isle of Wight History Centre, 2009 – http://www.iwhistory.org.uk/HER/0903antiaircraftbatteries.htm

8. The Home Guard records are archived in four boxes at the Isle of Wight Record Office, Newport – file ref. AC/87/75.

9. Cecil Faber Aspinall-Oglander (1878–1959), a veteran of the First World War, was a somewhat imperious Home Guard commander. Looking back in a letter written in 1973 on his years as commanding officer of 214 Infantry Brigade during its defensive assignment on the Isle of Wight, Major General Hubert Essame recalled that Aspinall-Oglander was 'inclined to be a bit awkward at times'.

Bibliography and Sources

Books

Allan, Dr Stuart – *Commando Country*, National Museums Scotland Enterprises, Edinburgh, 2007.

Banks, Sir Donald – *Flame over Britain*, Sampson Low, Marston & Co., London, 1946.

Churchill, Winston – *The Second World War Vol. II: Their Finest Hour*, Penguin Classics, London, 2005.

Dean, Mike – *Radar on the Isle of Wight*, Historical Radar Archive, Scampton, Lincs, 1994.

Dobinson, Colin – *Building Radar: Forging Britain's Early Warning Chain 1939–45*, Methuen Ltd., London, 2010.

Donnelly, Peter (editor) – *Mrs Milburn's Diaries: An Englishwoman's day-to-day reflections, 1939–1945*, George G. Harrap & Co., London, 1979.

Downing, Taylor – *Night Raid: The true story of the first victorious British para raid of WWII*, Little, Brown, London, 2013.

Ford, Ken – *The Bruneval Raid: Operating Biting 1942*, Osprey Publishing, Oxford, 2010.

Foynes, Julian – *The Battle of the East Coast*, Julian Foynes (self-published), 1994.

Haining, Peter – *Where the Eagle Landed: The mystery of the German invasion of Britain, 1940*, Robson Books, London, 2004.

Hayward, James – *The Bodies on the Beach: Sealion, Shingle Street and the burning sea myth of 1940*, CD41 Publishing, Dereham, Norfolk, 2001.

Hayward, James – *Myths and Legends of the Second World War*, The History Press, Stroud, Glos., 2009.

Jackson, Milenka (interviewer) – *Living Memory of the Jewish Community: Oskar Winter*, British Library National Life Story Collection, 1990.

Leal, H.J.T. – *Air War over the Island*, Isle of Wight County Press, 1982.

Leal, H.J.T. – *Battle in the Skies over the Isle of Wight*, Isle of Wight County Press, 1998.

Madej, W. Victor – *German Army Order of Battle: The Replacement Army, 1939–45*, Game Book Marketing Co., 1984.

Millar, George –*The Bruneval Raid: Flashpoint of the radar war*, Book Club Associates by arrangement with The Bodley Head, London, 1974.

Morison, Samuel Eliot – *The Invasion of France and Germany, 1944–45 (History of United States naval operations in World War II)*, Little, Brown & Co., New York (new edition, Castle Books, 2001).

Neilands, Robin – *By Land & By Sea: The Story of the Royal Marine Commandos*, Pen & Sword Books, Barnsley, Yorks., 2004.

Nudd, Derek –*Armageddon. Fed Up With This: A gunner's Tale*, self-published via Matador, Leicestershire, 2015.

Peake, Nigel – – *City at War: A pictorial memento of Portsmouth, Gosport, Fareham, Havant and Chichester during World War Two*, Milestone Publications, Portsmouth, 1986.

Scovell, Brian – *Thank you, Hermann Goering: The life of a sports writer,* Amberley Publishing, Stroud, Glos., 2010.

Searle, Adrian – *The Isle of Wight at War 1939–45,* The Dovecote Press, Wimborne, Dorset, 1989.

Smith, Peter C. – *Naval Warfare in the English Channel 1939–45,* Pen & Sword Books, Barnsley, South Yorks., 2007.

Toms, Jan – *The Little Book of the Isle of Wight,* The History Press, Slough, Glos., 2011.

Winton, John – *Death of the Scharnhorst,* Cassell Military Paperbacks, London, 2004.

Zimmerman, David – *Britain's Shield: Radar and the defeat of the Luftwaffe,* Amberley Publishing, Stroud, Glos., 2001.

Journals / Magazines

Hansard, London – The case of Dr Alfred Laurence, HL Deb. 21 May 1969 vol. 302 cc319-21.

Hansard, London – The case of Dr Alfred Laurence, HL Deb. 22 May 1969 vol. 302 cc490-3.

Island Life, Newport, Isle of Wight – The Island celebrates the end of six years of war with Germany, June Efford. 2009.

Radar Bulletin, London – Victory Souvenir Number, 1945 (reprinted by Historical Radar Archive, 1991).

RUSI Journal, London – Raids in the Last War and their Lessons, Major-General R.E. Laycock, November 1947.

Southampton Medical Journal – Carl Pauisnitz: Father of Clinical Allergy, David W. Hide, October 1992.

Newspapers

(various issues)

Daily Herald, London (defunct).

East Anglian Daily Times, Ipswich.

Eastern Daily Press, Cambridge.

Ipswich Star.

Isle of Wight County Press, Newport.

Isle of Wight Mercury, Ventnor (defunct).

The Times, London.

Television

BBC 1: *The One Show* (Shingle Street), 2014.

BBC East: *Inside Out,* (Shingle Street), 2002.

Discovery History: *Wartime Secrets with Harry Harris,* (Shingle Street), 2010.

Internet

Adams, Don – *Ventnor Radar,* www.ventnorradar.co.uk/

Barrett, Dick – *Ground Control Intercept (GCI),* www.radarpages.co.uk/mob/gci/gci.htm

Buckland, Ernest (Jim), via West Sussex Library Service – *Attempted German Invasion,* www.bbc.co.uk/history/ww2peopleswar/stories/17/a4213117.shtml

Cahill, Matthew – *Silencing Lord Haw-Haw: An analysis of British public reaction to the broadcasts, conviction and execution of Nazi propagandist William Joyce,* http://digitalcommons.wou.edu/his/46/

Commonwealth War Grave Commission – Cemetery Details, Isle of Wight (various), www.cwg/find-a-cemetery/

Commonwealth War Graves Commission – Casualties of the Auxiliary Territorial Service, www.atsremembered.org

Crofts, Jim, via BBC Southern Counties Radio – *A short break in transmission*, www.bbc.co.uk/history/ww2peopleswar/stories/60/a7151960.shtml

Forces War Records – Records Database, www.forces-war-records.co.uk

Frankfurter Personenlexicon – *Andernacht, Dietrich*, www.frankfurter-personenlexikon.de/node/4608

McNally, Brendan – *The Granville Raid*, www.defensemediaetwork.com/stories/the-geanville-raid

Subterranea Britannica – *Site Record: RAF St Lawrence – Chain Home Remote Reserve*, www.subbrit.org.uk/sb-sites/sites/s/st_lawrence_remote_reserve/

Young, Geoff – *4th Wilts soldier captured by E-boat crew*, www.bbc.co.uk/history/ww2peopleswa

Original sources

Bundesarchiv (Germany) – various records relating to special forces operations (1943).

Carisbrooke Castle Museum, Isle of Wight – Island at War 1974 exhibition documents (Philip Davis letter).

Cornwall's Regimental Museum, Bodmin – Duke of Cornwall's Light Infantry Regimental Histoty (5th DCLI).

Isle of Wight Record Office, Newport – IWECC ARP/L/11 (ARP records); AC/87/75 (Sandown Home Guard records).

National Archives, Kew – HO 207/1175 (Shingle Street evacuation, 1940); AVIA 26/1074 (TRE signals watch, RAF Ventnor, 1943); AIR 32/8 (Analysis of training, Operation Biting, 1942).

National Museum of the Royal Navy, Portsmouth – records relating to coastal patrols (1943).

RAF Museum, Hendon – X004-2321. (Betty Chadwick memoirs).

The Rifles (office), Taunton – Somerset Light Infantry regimental records (7th SLI).

Trinity House, London – records for St Catherine's lighthouse (1943).

Twining family correspondence, Isle of Wight, 1941 (RAF St Lawrence).

Index